IN OTHER WORDS

QUOTES THAT PUSH OUR THINKING

RACHELLE DENE POTH

In Other Words:
Quotes That Push Our Thinking
Rachelle Dene Poth

Published by EduMatch®
PO Box 150324, Alexandria, VA 22315
www.edumatch.org

Cover art by Hann Morrissey

These books are available at special discounts when purchased in quantities of 10 or
more for use as premiums, promotions fundraising, and educational use. For
inquiries and details, contact the publisher: sarah@edumatch.org.

JUDGING A BOOK BY ITS COVER

You might wonder why I chose the image I did for the cover of my book. I chose it because it was drawn by one of my students. Early on in the writing of this book, I noticed the sketchbook of one of my ninth graders and was amazed at the talent. Giving it some thought, I asked if Hann had an interest in drawing something for me to use. At that time, not considering it for the cover, but instead to include an authentic work of student art.

Had I not changed who I was as a teacher, I would not have likely noticed the sketchbook, nor interacted with the student to look at their work, to ask questions, or to ask them to draw something for me. Having changed my view of what it means to teach, I believe strongly in the building of relationships, of knowing our students and of letting them know us too.

I asked the question, "If I say the words creativity, curiosity, learning, and different, what would you draw?" A few days later, I received the cat drawing and I was amazed. I love so much of what it represents.

They say don't judge a book by its cover, but I want people to be drawn in by this book cover. For me, it is a symbol of change. It represents patience, curiosity, courage, flexibility, and an adventurous spirit.

DEDICATION

"Once we believe in ourselves, we can risk curiosity, wonder, spontaneous delight, or any experience that reveals the human spirit."

~ E.E. Cummings

To my family: David, Mom and Dad, and My 53s, thank you for your constant support, encouragement and for believing in me so that I could learn to believe in myself.

To the #4OCFPLN, thank you for being a part of this journey.

To Sarah-Jane Thomas, thank you for your guidance, inspiration, and for creating opportunities for educators and students around the world.

FOREWORD

Can one quote change your life?

I firmly believe the answer to be a resounding, "Yes."

In fact, I am an avid collector of quotes and, as Terri Guillemets wonderfully stated, "As a quotation collector, I collect wisdom, life, invisible beauty, souls alive in ink." Wow. "Souls alive in ink" is exactly how I want people to feel when they read my work. #Goals Don't be fooled into believing that small word count necessarily means small impact or lack of significance because often the exact opposite is true. It is the brevity that paradoxically makes them more powerful. As Willis Goth Regier said, "In phrases as brief as a breath wordly wisdom concentrates."

When making my final decision about whether to sign my book, Teach Like a PIRATE, away to a traditional publisher or start Dave Burgess Consulting Inc. with my wife Shelley, I came across a quote from Seth Godin that seared into my soul and echoed in my ears to the point of total distraction. Seth said, "Reject the tyranny of picked. Pick yourself." There it was. You don't have to be picked.

You don't have to be chosen. There is no need to raise your hand and wait to be called on in life. Pick yourself. Choose you. We politely declined all offers from the "big houses" and started a company on a laptop. That decision has been transformative for me, my family, and, ultimately, the educational publishing industry. One quote at exactly the right time changed everything.

That powerful potential is what lies within this book, *In Other Words*, by Rachelle Dene Poth. Rachelle has culled, curated, and compiled educational quotes that have led her down the path to tremendous insight, a paradigm shift, or changed her practice in a profound way. The real power comes in how she draws connections between these wise words and how they sparked a new direction in thinking that she then followed and expanded upon. In other words (pardon the pun), it was not so much the quote alone, but rather the reflective practice that holds the true power.

Rachelle is a master at this reflective practice and true role model for what it means to be a voracious and life-long learner. She is a Spanish teacher, a STEAM evangelist, has a master's degree in Instructional Technology, she's an attorney with a Juris Doctor Degree, a blogger, an author of multiple books, a contributing author to many more, a consultant, a professional development speaker, an active member and leader of too many educational organizations to name, all the while being a prolific connector and sharer on social media. Her resume is lengthy, impressive, and only surpassed by her proclivity to shine the light on her colleagues and her students instead of herself. In this very spirit, numerous educators from her professional learning network have contributed their insights to the book and share quotes that have transformed their practice. In addition, since student voice and authentic student learning are so central to her passions as an educator, there is a chapter of student contributions, and even the cover of this beautiful book was created by a student. Rachelle walks the talk.

It is my hope that somewhere inside this book you will find a quote that changes your educational journey for the better or that it will lead you to become connected to someone who may transform your life. One quote…sometimes that's all it takes.

Dave Burgess

New York Times Best Selling author of *Teach Like a PIRATE*

President of Dave Burgess Consulting, Inc.

PREFACE: OUR STORIES

Throughout this book, you will hear stories from educators with different backgrounds and different roles in education. I hope that by sharing *our* stories, we will inspire you to share *yours*.

CONTENTS

INTRODUCTION

I AM A PART OF EVERYTHING I HAVE READ.

TEDDY ROOSEVELT

Teddy Roosevelt once said, "I am a part of everything I have read." This quote greatly resonates with me, specifically focusing on the past five years as I have become a more avid reader, especially when it comes to books related to education, and for personal and professional growth. I have always enjoyed reading, but the types of books that interest me have changed with time and varied depending on whether I had any choice in deciding what book to read.

As a kid, I didn't mind the readers we had for school. Although the storylines were at times repetitive and often boring, I still enjoyed them. Why? Because I loved learning to read and developing my own curiosity and experiencing the success of finishing a book. My childhood favorites came down to two book collections: *Paddington Bear* by Michael Bond and any book by Judy Blume, author of *Are you there God? It's me Margaret*, which was a favorite for many of us in the sixth grade. There was also a period when I started reading Harlequin romance novels. Surprising right? Thinking about it now, I am not sure why I wanted to, but I remember going to local thrift shops or garage sales with my mom and buying the books for a quarter. I think I was just excited that I could buy a book with my spare change. I don't remember actually reading those Harlequin books, maybe I just flipped through some of the pages and collected them to look like I was reading. As a kid, sometimes my habits were strange.

No doubt, my choices were an interesting combination of books for a sixth grader — far apart in terms of content, but works of fiction, based on imagination and creativity, and fun to read. Even though they were works of fiction, they often included real-world facts or explored issues that children might be learning about or experiencing. I remember reading through them so fast, eager to start the next book, but often there was no next book yet. So that meant a weekend trip to the library with my parents, where I would spend an hour in the children's section looking for something that might compare to those books. It was a struggle because I wanted the same kind of books. Perhaps a little narrow-minded, I didn't want to branch out and read books from other authors. Regardless of what teachers or friends would recommend, I would look at almost every book on the shelves trying to find something that looked similar. I eventually found Beverly Cleary, and that at least gave me some options until my favorite authors wrote new books.

Lessons Learned from Reading as a Child:

1. Reading is fun,
2. Reading pushes your imagination, and

3. Reading opens up different worlds of learning.

In high school, I don't remember reading books because *I chose* to read them. The books I read were books chosen *for* me or required for my English courses. I remember frequently struggling with understanding the themes or underlying meaning behind them, which usually meant a trip to the bookstore with my parents to buy Cliff's Notes. I also understood more by talking about them with my dad, who had read a lot of the same books and was able to help me understand a bit more. As for the Cliff's Notes (the non-tech version of SparkNotes), I didn't use them to avoid doing the reading. I used them to better understand after I finished reading the book. Reading in high school was much different than reading as a child. It wasn't just reading for fun anymore, at least it did not feel like it. There was more to it. We had to dissect the meaning, the theme, the point of view, evaluate characters, understand what the author was trying to convey, identify syntax and recognize protagonists, and so much more. There were outlines to complete, vocabulary words to define, and essays to write. It was more challenging; we were held accountable for the content and having a more in-depth understanding, and I did not find it to be as much fun, nor did I understand a lot of it. Except for maybe ninth grade English — I still remember the books, and although they were based on fiction, they included historical and geographical information. This helped me to transfer knowledge to my other courses and begin to understand things more.

Lessons Learned from Reading in High School:

1. Sometimes we all need to read the same book to understand different perspectives and push our critical thinking skills.
2. We can read the same book but get a different story. I often tell students how much I enjoyed reading *Great*

Expectations, which shocks many of them (current students who did not like reading it in their English classes). Their shock doubles whenever I add that I also enjoyed *A Tale of Two Cities* and *The Old Man and The Sea* (books my dad gave me to read and that we discussed, also apparently not favorites of current high school students).

3. By reading, we learn about things besides English. There was something about these books that helped me beyond the skills I was building in writing and vocabulary. I learned about different places, historical facts, geography, and reinforced my learning in other content areas that were difficult for me to master.

College reading meant French novels and books related to education like *Savage Inequalities* by Jonathan Kozol and *All I Need to Know I Learned in Kindergarten* by Robert Fulghum. When I had time, I enjoyed reading novels by Mary Higgins Clark and John Grisham. Again, like when I was a child, I only wanted books from these authors. People would offer to lend me a book to read, often a mystery or a legal book similar to the Clark and Grisham styles, but I didn't want them because I knew they wouldn't compare. These books were similar: fiction, with some real-world connections to history and geography, lots of legal procedure talk, and they pushed my critical thinking and problem-solving skills. Building these skills meant analyzing the text, and trying to understand the underlying theme, tone, and other literary elements. Sometimes I needed the Cliff's Notes to make sense of it, but only after reading the book passages a few times first. I soon realized there would be no shortcuts for learning.

After college graduation, I did not read many books. Between teaching and working on my Spanish degree, the reading that I did was limited to the stories that my students were reading in class or those required for my own coursework. When I went to law school, my reading involved giant casebooks and study guide materials.

Lessons Learned:

1. Sometimes we have to read books that we may not want to, but need to believe that the underlying purpose is to help us grow.
2. The more we read, the better we write, the better we can communicate.
3. Everyone makes mistakes. Making mistakes is how we learn. Take some risks with learning and embrace the mistakes and keep moving forward.

Reading That Changed Me

There are books that changed my thinking and pushed me to change my actions — books that led me to rethink my purpose as an educator and to find my passion. Why did I not know about these books sooner?

I never really read books about education after college, until I came across a hashtag on Twitter for "#tlap." I figured out that it referred to the book *Teach Like a Pirate* by Dave Burgess. During the summer of 2015, as I traveled by Amtrak across the state to attend my first ISTE (International Society for Technology in Education) Conference in Philadelphia, I started and finished "TLAP" during the train ride. This book led me to really question who I was as a teacher. What kind of teacher had I been? I thought that I had been doing a lot — fun activities, games, and more — but I realized that what I had been doing in my classroom was not enough. It was easy; I had used similar materials, methods, and had a routine. I needed to do more and to be more for my students. I started with *Teach Like a Pirate*, which led me to find more books about education, books which have inspired me to change. Had I not started and continued, I would still be teaching the way I was: in isolation and afraid of taking risks.

Since reading *Teach Like a Pirate* (Burgess, 2015), I have read many books related to education, technology, and professional growth, and have a never-ending stack in my "to be read" pile. My childhood problem of running out of books and pickiness for authors has been resolved; my passion for reading and my passion for learning has continued to grow.

Lessons Learned from Reading TLAP:

1. Be curious about learning.
2. Be a risk-taker and don't settle for doing things the traditional way. *Be different!*
3. Be vulnerable. Share your story. Inspire others to act.

THE IMPORTANT THING IS NOT TO STOP QUESTIONING. CURIOSITY HAS ITS OWN REASON FOR EXISTING. – ALBERT EINSTEIN

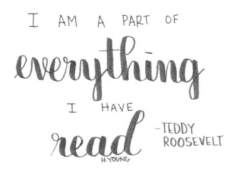

Like Teddy Roosevelt, I am a part of everything I have read. From childhood until now, the books I have chosen and the books which have been chosen for me have left some mark or imprint in my mind. I still remember where I got most of my books, who read books to me, and have distinct memories attached to certain books. Over the past five years, many books have pushed me to think differently, as well as to grow professionally and personally. My "takeaways" from these books, have been quotes that I've committed to memory. Quotes which push my thinking, lift me when I need it, and remind me to keep reaching for more and always to be reflective in my practice.

I've always loved quotes and use them either to motivate myself or to inspire or encourage others. Some quotes have a special meaning to me, whether they lead me to feeling nostalgic, give me the courage to push through a challenge I am facing, or enable me to connect with someone else. We can interpret quotes in personal and authentic ways, which perhaps inspire us to take action, to be brave, or to do something differently. Quotes can remind us to keep perspective and stay positive or help us to understand something in a different way.

When starting this writing project, I had accumulated a lot of quotes from four years of reading, exploring, and seeking inspiration. Throughout this book, many quotes reflect the theme of each chapter and are related to education — quotes which have inspired me and given me strength when I needed it. My own experiences and interpretations and the educator vignettes shared by my PLN (Personal or Professional Learning Network) will hopefully push your thinking, inspire you, and provide whatever it is that you need.

In *Dare to Lead*, Brené Brown wrote, "write the book you need to read." Writing and compiling these stories has been a fantastic experience that has led me down an incredible path of reflection, self-awareness, and professional growth.

Throughout this book, you will hear from many different educators and even two of my students. There are vignettes shared within each chapter as well as guest chapters, where each author shares their interpretation of a quote and how it has applied to their work as an educator and their own personal life.

While the original author of the quote conveys a specific message and has enlightened the reader in some way, the reader may interpret it, *"In other words..."*

PART I

"It's not so much what we have in this life that matters. It's what we do with what we have." — Fred Rogers

Chapter 1

COURAGE

The Beginning

---

*"Vulnerability is not winning or losing; it's having the **courage** to show up and be seen when we have no control over the outcome."*

— *Brené Brown*

L ife can be challenging. We all have our own stressors, and sometimes the smallest thing can lead to the most significant response in terms of causing stress or awakening fear in us. It's weird how the mind and the body work, if you take a moment to sit back and think about all the different things that we experience each day. Minute by minute, hour by hour, there are so many things that can pop up in the blink of an eye, and somehow, we can process and react to these triggers instantly, without really taking time to think. Or do we?

There have been many times in my life where I felt pretty good about a challenge that I was facing and recall having moments of calmness where I could think about it clearly, had confidence, while building myself up to face it. But at times, this confidence and composure quickly disappeared because of a phenomenon that I learned about while reading *Escaping the School Leader's Dunk Tank* by Rick Jetter and Rebecca Coda. This phenomenon referred to as "proactive paranoia" is something that we all experience. Jetter and Coda define it as the "anticipation of problems, negative reactions or responses of others" (pp. 9-11) — a "healthy" type of paranoia that helps us to "get ready for battle." I think of it as the little voice inside of my head, the one that sometimes I cannot quiet down. It can either propel us forward and prepare us, or perhaps talk us out of something before we even think about going for it. This little voice can do so much damage so quickly, fed by insecurities, self-doubt, and the need to protect oneself. It's one thing when someone else tells you that you can't do something. I have strong feelings about this and do not like to be told that I can't (or hear someone else being told that they can't) do something. But it's another thing entirely when you are the one putting up a wall, closing yourself off to any possibility for learning and growing, backing out because of fear rather than taking time to breathe, to refocus, and to go for it. You listen to that voice too often. I listen to that voice too often. It gets the best of me.

I don't know where the fear comes from, or how to make it disappear. When we think about our lives, I hope that we have each had far more successes than failures, and that those failures in some way have led us to successes. We need to use failure as an opportunity to reevaluate and challenge ourselves to do better. Keeping ourselves stagnant, perhaps afraid to get out there and do things differently and think differently, because that voice of self-doubt tells us not to, would be the biggest failure of all. More than that, especially in our role as educators and leaders, if we are stopping ourselves from pushing for change and facing challenges, we are limiting the students and colleagues over whom we have influence. We cannot let that happen. Perhaps easier said than done, but because of one quote, I have a constant reminder that pushes me to give something a few more tries before I back down, bail out, and run away from the challenge — but only after I have already convinced myself that I can't. Proactive Paranoia.

I Can't Do It

It started with an intense fear of public speaking. In the summer of 2017, I had three events where I would have to give a keynote or speak to a large audience. I have spoken at many other events to different sized audiences, sometimes to a mix of people I know or to complete strangers in other states and conferences, but I have developed a bit of fear. You might laugh, but one of the first things I tend to say whenever I have to speak, whether it's a keynote or a small group presentation, is that I really don't like public speaking. For many years in our school professional development sessions, I would have gladly done any activity other than being the spokesperson for the group that I was in. There was just something about speaking in front of my peers that scared me. It was the worst experience that I could imagine. I could feel it physically and mentally. The anxiety that would start when I'd catch myself thinking that I might actually have to say something in front of everyone. It's that feeling you get when something happens quickly, like you just missed having an accident, or you catch yourself from falling, and you can feel the tingles of nerves shooting throughout your body. It takes a while to shake it off. Same thing for me. Even if I think I might have a somewhat decent idea to share or something to contribute, I still struggle with speaking in front of others.

You see, along with that voice that tells me that I *can't* do something, that "proactive paranoia," I also struggle with self-confidence in my abilities or expressing my thoughts. Sometimes the doubt creeps in that my thoughts don't have any value or would not be helpful to others. I don't know why this happens to any of us, but it is something that I know has been part of my personality and character for many years, if not my whole life. While I recognize it, I have yet to conquer it and control it completely, but I am getting better. By channeling my believed weaknesses and fears and instead focusing on trying to encourage others to face their own, I push back my own fears. Booker T. Washington stated, "If we want to lift ourselves, lift someone else up," and I believe that completely and aspire to do this more every day.

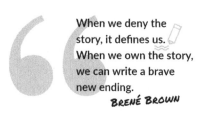

When we deny the story, it defines us. When we own the story, we can write a brave new ending.
BRENÉ BROWN

@SteinbrinkLaura

"When we deny the story, it defines us. When we own the story, we can write a brave new ending." — Brené Brown

Jeff Kubiak
Elementary School Principal
California
@jeffreykubiak

Choices. Actions. Words. They begin and end with us. As we move ahead in life, we either accept what is under our control, or dismiss it and face a possible repercussion.

As an educator, there are many days where I have to write a new story ending continuously. I own my mistakes, my challenges, and my choices. As I lead and learn with both adults and students, I, in turn, must face the waves of change, head-on.

By denying our story, we are refusing to grow. Disputing change. Holding on to our past. And some still try to latch on to one last strand of the rope of what may have worked or had been successful before. This will only hold us back and be a detriment to our children.

Grab for the wind my friends — you may not get a hold of it this time, but someday, you'll write about how you did, and the great things that happened because of it.

———

YOU MIGHT THINK that you're alone in something that you are experiencing, but how will you ever honestly know if you don't share your story? Know who you are. Be confident, and in those moments when you feel down or like you just can't catch a break, use those thoughts to lift someone else.

Heather Lippert
Kindergarten Teacher
Cedar Valley Community School
@msyoung114

On an August day, my classroom was terribly warm, and I thought about taking off my cardigan sweater. If I took off my sweater, my short-sleeved shirt would reveal the tattoos on my arms to my new kindergarten families that I would be meeting for the first time. Would they judge me as unfit to teach their children because of the art on my arms? Would they view me as a bad influence?

I considered putting the sweater back on and sweating through the meetings but then realized — I don't have control over the first impressions the families will have of me.

I took the sweater off and pushed the thoughts out of my head. My families came into the classroom, and I learned about them and their children. All I could do was be my authentic self and take time throughout the year to show my families the care, love, and academic growth I weave into my practice. As teachers, it's essential that we find the courage to take off the sweater and let our true selves be seen in our classrooms every day.

JOE
SANFELIPPO

Share Who You Are & Be Vulnerable

As educators, we know it's who we are and what we do that can make a difference in the lives of others. We impact not just our students, but also our colleagues and the families that we interact with. We can't ever truly know the impact of our work, but we need to be mindful that we are in a position that places us under a watchful eye, even when we don't realize it — ears that hear what we say, even when we think we're not speaking loudly. And actions speak louder than words, so our body language, the mannerisms, gestures, facial expressions, and the slightest exhale of air can all convey so much at any given moment. We might unknowingly convey a message that someone picks up on, and we don't realize the impact, good or bad that it may have. In *Hacking Leadership* (2017), Joe Sanfelippo wrote, "In the absence of knowledge, people make up their own." This quote is a good reminder that we need to be mindful of all the things which can make us vulnerable to others telling our stories for us. We need to tell our own.

There are different meanings of vulnerable, some of which might suggest that it's something that shows a sign of weakness or places someone in a position of disadvantage. However, what I have learned is that it's okay to be vulnerable and to show our vulnerability to others. Vulnerability is not a sign of weakness; it is actually a sign of strength. Having the strength to show that we may not have all the answers, we are taking a risk, we made a mistake, or we just lost our composure are just some of the examples of what we can experience showing our vulnerability. I think it's so important as educators that we not only share our experiences with our students or with those with whom we work, but that we talk openly about it and show that it's okay to be vulnerable. We will face challenges and have things that do not necessarily go as we planned. It's what we do after we expose our vulnerability that matters and that defines us.

YOU MUST DO THE THINGS
YOU THINK YOU CANNOT DO.
— ELEANOR ROOSEVELT

@MANUELHERRERA55

When I think about Brown's quote about vulnerability, it reminds me of those keynotes and speaking events in 2017, where I wanted to bail out. I don't know that I've ever felt that much worry or anxiety other than possibly while in law school. But this was a different kind of feeling — one which was starting to consume me completely. It was all that I could think about. I tried to talk myself down from the high level of doubt that I was feeling. I knew that I could not back out, or perhaps more correctly stated, that I *should* not back out. Why? Because that is not an example to set for students. Eleanor Roosevelt said, "Do one thing every day that scares you." I think that is absolutely true. We can't keep living in the comfortable areas of our life. While that may make us feel better and reduce our worry temporarily, it does not help us to grow and do better or be better.

The quote from Brené Brown comes from her book *Daring Greatly*, the title of which is based on a speech given by Teddy Roosevelt, in which he talked about how there are people who want to see others fail and fall. And that even though a person may enter into a battle or is facing a challenge; if success happens, that's great. But if failure results, then you failed while daring greatly. We need to keep this in our minds, and it is something that the voice in our head needs to learn to say and to repeat often. We should strive to not only push through our own challenges, but also to help others push through theirs as well. It goes along with this idea of being vulnerable and being mindful of keeping perspective. It's okay to feel like you have the weight of the world on your shoulders. Have you been told things like "don't make mountains out of molehills," and "don't sweat the small stuff," but what you are experiencing feels anything but small? You feel like you are experiencing the worst. Chances may be high that what we are going through is not that big of a deal compared to what others go through. But we all live in our own space and sometimes the smallest thing to others might feel like an insurmountable challenge to us. We shouldn't discredit the feelings of others, even if we don't necessarily under-stand why something seems to be so challenging to them. We need to remember that everyone experiences challenges — some big, some small, and some that you cannot even quantify, but we cannot take away, belittle, or think lowly of others who might be so afraid of something that to us, seems like nothing at all.

And while it is essential to recognize and face our fears, we also need to remember to take a moment to talk ourselves down, to look around, to reflect, and regain our perspective. Are things really so bad? Or is our fear feeding it? Is the "proactive paranoia" talking and making something out of nothing much at all? There have been many times throughout my life where I feel like I just want to quit.

Moments where I believe that I won't be able to do something in time, or I am not "good enough." Sometimes I even start to back away from the challenge. It's easier not to try, rather than to try and fail, and be disappointed. But when I take time to pause, think through what I believe to be my challenge, and then try to relate it to something else I have experienced, many times I find that what has been scaring me is not so scary at all.

The more we focus on the negative or listen to the fear, the higher the likelihood is that we will continue to talk ourselves out of things that we are very much capable of doing. The key is finding a way to drown out that fear — to talk over it and convince yourself in fact that you can. This may not be the best way, but it doesn't matter because trying and failing is far better than not trying at all.

I'm sure we can all remember times in our life when we have struggled, whether facing fears or dealing with challenges. I've learned to use these experiences to remind myself that I can work through new struggles, as I have done in the past. Think about your own friends and family, or even stories you have heard about others and what they have faced, as a reminder to always keep perspective and to not focus on negativity or self-doubt so much. We all deal with adversities in our own way. It's important to remember that while we may struggle and experience fear and defeat, we're not alone. We only need to find a way to push through and use our experience to help others. We need to be okay asking for help when we need it.

"Be strong enough to stand alone, smart enough to know when you need help, and brave enough to ask it."

– Ziad K. Abdelnour, American Financier and Philanthropist

Kristen Nan
Educator
Pittsburgh, PA
@nankr1120

There is so much truth behind this quote when it comes to defining my journey in education, not just as a teacher, but as a student and person too. My notorious risk-taking has been positively infectious and detrimental all in the same right. It doesn't always run smoothly or come without consequence, but disrupting the status quo by adding color to a very black and white experience in education has been worth standing alone. I am one that thrives on being uncomfortable as stagnancy equates boredom for me. This shows up in all facets of my learning, as I focus on the journey and not necessarily the outcome. Being strong enough to stand alone was and never is by choice, but more a stubborn refusal to push forward towards a brighter tomorrow.

I am a survivor of circumstance to which I do not define myself nor do I self-pity. I have a strong belief in my convictions and a mindset willing to face harsh judgment for not following the safe path to which others may gravitate. I am a collaborator by nature, so asking for help and appreciating that others are available and willing has never been a fear of mine, and in most ways intrigues me. In the big picture, I think that the trifecta of this quote is what has been to my detriment.

There are all types of people in this world, and most often human nature is drawn to the comfort of similar traits and overall identity. The toughest for me typically mirrors the antithesis of my strength. My independence and willingness to take a risk, fail, and find value in the journey can often intimidate those who question themselves, stay within their comfort zone, and find fear in failure. I am not that person. My need is for betterment at all times. For me, I have always been drawn towards better... better than me... better than my today. I have always thrived on knowing what better looks like, feels like, and what it would take to create it with my own ambition and belief. This to me is beyond bravery, but more of a glimpse into wisdom.

You don't belong here, or do you?

By applying to and then attending law school while still teaching full-time, there were people watching to see how I would do. Some were actually hoping to see me fail, which bothered me, but I realized that the only things that I could control were my own actions and preparation moving forward. Of course, I was worried about my ability to take on so much, but once I got started, I knew that I had to keep going no matter what. I had too much on the line at that point (family adjustments, financial investment, teaching career), that backing out was not an option (even though it was, or could have been).

One of the first lessons that I learned about being vulnerable was early in my law school career. I had to present an oral argument to a group of third- and fourth-year law students and professors whom I did not know, and it really intimidated me. While I had been confident in the argument practices, that confidence came from knowing there were only going to be six or seven people in the room, and I had spent time in class getting to know them. However, at this next stage, there would be other law students and professors, sitting in a formal courtroom. I remember being terrified and feeling so much pressure. For a long time, and especially that day, I felt like I didn't belong, that I was not meant to be there, that I didn't have what it took to make it through law school.

Support and Belonging

My parents attended the oral arguments that day and were very positive about how I had done. While I greatly appreciated their support and words of encouragement before and after my argument, they are my parents, and of course, they will give me positive feedback. Having my parents there made a big difference for me because, for the first time, I felt more confident and like I belonged. I was proud to have them be a part of it and see what I had been learning and to give me some validation that maybe I did belong.

Something else that changed for me that day and that continues to have an impact on me still was a brief interaction with one of the law professors. When I finished with my argument, this particular professor told me that I did a good job and should feel proud of myself. I can't recall that I ever had a teacher say that to me any time as a student, and this man was not even a professor of a class that I was taking. He didn't know me, but he took the time to step out and offer me some words of encouragement. That was one of the defining moments that will stay with me forever. Why? Because besides surviving that oral argument experience, even though I was convinced that everyone knew how nervous I was, I had some validation. With my parents there, it was an acknowledgment of what I had been investing my time in, and I also had the encouragement given by this professor. These combined to let me know that I could do this. I was meant to be there, just like everyone else. I just needed to start believing it, and no matter what, I would have to continue to put myself out there, challenge myself to do more, and to listen less to that confidence-stealing voice in my head telling me that I would not succeed. I needed to learn to speak over it to tell myself that I could. And more importantly, I learned two valuable lessons: One, to interact with all students, not just those in my classroom. Make time to connect and be supportive. Two, I learned the value of mentors.

The Merriam-Webster dictionary definition of vulnerability is "the quality or state of being exposed to the possibility of being attacked or harmed, either physically or emotionally." The word derives from the Latin verb *vulnerare,* meaning "to wound." It has been used figuratively since the late 1600s, to suggest "defenselessness against non-physical attacks." Non-physical attacks would be when someone is vulnerable to criticism or failure, or feels helpless or weak. Even though the word itself refers to a weakness, being vulnerable and sharing our vulnerabilities are far from being weak. We are all vulnerable.

Vulnerability and its Benefits in the Classroom

As educators, we need to show our vulnerability as a model for our students. We need to convey the message that it's okay to put yourself out there and take risks, face challenges, and sometimes even fall. This helps us to develop the resilience we need to work through our own challenges. We may never really know the extent of the personal challenges of the students who enter our classrooms and our schools, but the only way to help them to open up, to connect, and to provide the support they greatly need is by modeling vulnerability. We must lead the way.

We start by spreading the message that it's normal to struggle sometimes, and that being vulnerable is not a sign of weakness, but rather, a sign of strength. Putting ourselves out there and being able to recognize and then acknowledge that we need help is a sign of inner strength, a demonstration of self-awareness and the recognition of one's own needs. When students understand that they are not alone, that even their teachers have struggled and continue to struggle with different aspects of life, it helps to create an environment in which students can develop and thrive. They can invest their time more in learning and growing as a person and a student, rather than wasting time worrying about possible failures and struggles. We can replace their worry and instead embrace vulnerability by providing a supportive, risk-taking encouraged environment.

Bianca Bass said, "Never forget that everyone you've ever met has worried about failing at something. The difference is that some people—the people whose stories you have heard and applauded—chose to start anyway. We're all scared, and we're all making it up as we go along. So, start and start now."

What can you do today that will make an impact tomorrow?

"In the absence of knowledge, people make up their own."

— *Joe Sanfelippo*

Paul O'Neill
Educator
New Jersey
@pauloneill1972

Friend and colleague Bethany Hill taught me the power of

telling my own story. One of my personal and professional weaknesses has always been talking about myself. I'd rather shine the spotlight on someone else than turn the attention on myself. It's not that I'm a shy person. My preference has always been to let others do the talking. This quote speaks to me on many levels. I've seen personal as well as professional examples of people creating their own narratives in the absence of knowledge. This is a dangerous practice that can create significant misconceptions and chaos. So, be your own narrator and sing your story loudly and proudly.

CHALLENGE: SHARE AN EXPERIENCE THAT HAS DEFINED YOU IN SOME WAY AS AN EDUCATOR.

#QUOTES4EDU

Chapter 2

RELATIONSHIPS: KNOW OURSELVES TO KNOW OTHERS

---

*"What is best for this **learner**?" — George Couros*

When we think about our classrooms and students today, we can no longer only think specifically about teaching the class or designing activities for the class to do. We need to look closely at our classrooms and see each student to understand their respective needs and interests. As a high school student, I recall receiving the same assignment as everyone else in my class, including students in different class periods. To the best of my knowledge, there was not any personalization or differentiation back then, at least not that was recognizable to us as students, or that I can identify now looking back. I remember everyone having the same work to do each night (typically a worksheet, an outline, or crosswords for each of the 50 states that we did in the eighth grade). Just by asking our friends, we got a pretty good idea of what to expect going into the class because it was always the same.

When I started teaching, I based my practices on my own experiences as a student, avoiding things that I did not like, such as alphabetically assigned seats, or grading with a red pen. But when it came to teaching world language classes, I used the same methods in my own classroom for many years because I thought that the teaching methods used were the reason for my success. I believed what worked well for me would work for my students, and that I should do the same things my own teachers did. I thought that I needed to give a homework assignment every night, a quiz every week, a test at the end of every unit, and assign similar projects. I kept everything consistent. Each student did the same tasks in the same order, and I didn't think about changing it too much. At least not until one parent phone call.

About 15 years ago, I received a call from a parent who was concerned about the "amount" of homework being given in my class. While at first, you might think this sounds familiar because there has been a lot of talk and controversy about the appropriate (if any) amount of homework and the value of the homework itself, the real reason for the call was that there was *not enough* homework being given to the students — more specifically, to one student. I remember the call as though it happened last week. The problem was that one of my French students would complete the assignment within minutes of receiving it, before the period even ended, leaving nothing in the form of official homework to be done at home. The parent was concerned that I was not giving enough homework and suggested that I provide extra practice for students because this quick finishing of the homework should not happen. There had to be something done at home, some form of practice or way for parents to see that the students were learning and applying what they were learning.

It definitely led me to think about the homework that I had been assigning. Was it too much, too repetitive, or too little? I tried to be more cognizant of homework practices from then on. I asked students how long it took them to complete the assignments and tried to find some middle ground. It was hard to break away from the way I had been doing things, ways that I thought led to greater learning (because they did for me). Having students copy words multiple times, translate sentences and paragraphs, complete workbook pages and packets, were all things I had done as a student. But I was not considering the benefit nor impact of these practices on my own students. What did they need?

I took the time to observe, ask, and listen. Some students struggled with specific assignments, sometimes taking 30 minutes or longer to complete a worksheet. And for others, that same assignment was completed within five to ten minutes. I tried to close that gap by adjusting some of the assignments and trying to think through them better than I had been doing. But I wish I had realized back then that it wasn't about the individual assignment itself, but rather providing opportunities for enrichment or additional practice, and more choices in learning.

I needed to move away from a one-size-fits-all approach to homework that was not fitting for all students. More conversations should have happened back then with the students to find out about their interests and their misunderstandings, how they learned best, how they preferred to study, and other essential considerations like these. It comes down to the relationships and finding out firsthand what each student needs. But I was not doing this, because I did not realize that it was okay to interact with the students and have conversations focused on things beyond merely the content. I didn't think of asking them about their learning styles or preferences, because I had never been asked when I was a student. I just assumed that teachers made the decisions and that students complied, without having any choices. I was wrong. It was something that I should have done, but I didn't know that it would be a good teaching practice. I didn't realize the impact that it could have on student learning.

Every Student, Every Day

When we think about preparing our classrooms for our students today, our focus shouldn't be "what am I going to teach the *class*?" We must move away from delivering content to all students in the same format because our students deserve authentic and personalized learning opportunities. What we need to ask ourselves should be more along the lines of, "What am I hoping to cover in class and how am I going to teach it or relate that to *each* of my students? How am I going to present it so that all students can interpret it in their own unique way that makes the most sense to them?"

This is not how I had been teaching. I had no idea of the difference when I started, so it took me a while to recognize that I needed to make some changes. Part of me was oblivious to the fact that it was okay to do things differently, that I did not need to provide the same experience for each student. If it took some students longer to complete a task, then the rest of the class waited. I also thought that everything I was doing was "right" and that the students needed to adjust to my style. But my teaching style was not working like I thought it should be. I started to have difficulties finding ways to engage students in learning, and I wanted to do more than just talk at them and assign worksheets. Students need to practice, but they don't all need the same kind. Finding alternate forms of practice and offering examples for students to try out on their own are just a few of the first steps that I took. These are good ideas to start with until you feel more comfortable, have time to interact with students, and learn some of the ways that help them to interpret the content.

It is definitely a challenge to cover all of the content that we are supposed to each year while making sure we meet the needs of each student. Class periods typically do not provide enough time for teachers to work with each student regularly. One of the best ways to defeat the time problem is by mixing things up. One September morning, I decided that I had enough of the rows of desks and moved them into stations within my room. I took a risk and broke away from the traditional ways I had been teaching. The breakdown of rows was the first; next was getting rid of my scripted daily lesson plans. Many times, when I came up with an idea for the class, it likely was something I thought up moments before the students entered the classroom. Other times it might have been an idea that I found by talking to a colleague or looking online at teacher resources and doing my best to apply it in a way that I thought might work for my students.

I know that whatever I ultimately decided to do would be a risk but that it would be one well worth taking in the interest of students. Some people might think teaching is easy, and in some ways, it can be. If you really love what you do and enjoy investing your time and yourself into the "work," then because of the deep commitment you have to your students, it probably doesn't feel like work at all. But the reality of it is that teaching today is tough. There are days where both you and the students might feel frustrated and struggle to get through the day. Perhaps because of a lack of progress in covering some of the material, trying a new idea and it not going as planned, feeling like there's just too much to cover, or students showing signs of becoming overwhelmed, frustrated, or confused. And you might be feeling overwhelmed too. It happens.

We have so many responsibilities in addition to our roles as teachers. This is why it is so important to work on relationships by making time to break away from the content, have some fun with learning, talk with students, and then get back to the lessons. We must strive to be the positive forces in the day for our students, but we also know that sometimes it's the students who have the positive impact on us.

> *"It's the little conversations that build the relationships and make an impact on each student."* — Robert John Meehan

HAVE you ever gone into your classroom and you already feel drained — wishing the day would go fast, feeling like you need a day off, or questioning how you're going to make it through? Some days I have thoughts of taking half of a sick day: the pressure builds, the headache comes on, and I convince myself that I won't get through the day. But once students arrive, those feelings disappear, and I feel almost rejuvenated. I'm sure some can relate to this; I know there are days where I wake up, and I'm excited to get to school. Then as I start the drive in, that excitement becomes clouded by thoughts of all of the tasks that I need to accomplish during the day, and I lose sight of my real purpose.

So how do we handle it all? By doing what's best for our students and being mindful of any limits on what we can reasonably hope to cover and engage students in each day. It's important to find balance for ourselves and not take on so much. It's easy to become so passionate about teaching and learning that we wear ourselves out trying some new technology tool or finding ways to implement one of the buzzword trends out there in education, just because it seems like the thing to do. We become afraid to say "no," as though it will make us a less caring and invested teacher. In order to be our best selves for students, we need to remember that it's not just about us and what *we* bring to the classroom —

our students should be involved in making decisions for *our* class too.

Building classroom connections and understanding each student must be a priority each day. The only way this can happen is by making time to get to know students, beginning on day one and working on it every day. Start by greeting students at the door, engaging in conversations, and taking that critical time to build connections and grow your classroom climate and culture. The content and curriculum can wait another day or two. What can't wait is getting to know the students and understanding how to best help each and every one of them.

"Every student can learn, just not on the same day and not in the same way." — *George Evans*

Paul O'Neill
Educator
New Jersey
@pauloneill1972

One of the most wonderful things about our profession is the fact that everyone learns differently. As educators, our greatest challenge is finding ways to differentiate the learning experience for each one of our learners. A common misconception about differentiation is that we must focus on strategies to assist our most struggling and reluctant learners. What does that mean for learners who are at or above grade level? Now, more than ever, we must plan, prepare and deliver learning experiences that encourage students to stretch themselves. By using the power of inquiry, we can reinforce learning, ignite curiosity, and collect data that can be used to increase student achievement.

When I was in school...

Think back to when you were in school. Maybe that was only five or ten years ago, or perhaps it was longer like 20, 30, or more. What was your classroom experience like? Were you asked about how you learn best or given choices about how to show your learning? Did you openly share your feelings about any of the assignments or projects that you were asked to do? For example, did you tell your teacher that it was a waste of your time or ask why you had to do it?

Or did you just accept the work that you had been given, without question, and do what you had been asked to do? The work I had in my high school years was quite demanding, and I struggled through many assignments.

Now I can probably look back and recognize that the assignments might not have been the best formats for practice, at least for me and my needs, but I believe that my teachers were doing what they thought was best. At that time, it meant providing all students with pretty much the same assignment and using the drill and practice method. This included having students' complete tasks such as copying vocabulary multiple times, defining new words, and other similar activities that were intended to provide a repetitive way of learning the material. There are times I can recall outlining chapter after chapter in a history or science course, and spending hours in the evening trying to complete these tasks and struggling — not because of the material, but because I did not know the proper format to use for creating an outline. Sometimes it was the little things that got in the way of my actual learning of the content. I wonder how many other students struggled with this part of the task like I did.

Do you remember having the same assignment as your peers, perhaps understanding the content but finding it difficult to apply it to whatever the homework assignment was? Or worse, unable to show what you had learned on a test? Personally, I remember many times struggling to complete worksheets for math or history class. I loved to read, but often had a hard time answering the reading comprehension questions for a book we were reading in class, especially those that asked for a more in-depth analysis of theme or tone. Sometimes I just couldn't show my learning in the exact way that I was being asked to.

If instead, you asked me questions about any of those subjects, chances are that I could have given you answers and explained my thoughts and demonstrated my understanding in more complex ways. But being given a worksheet with specific questions and answers and having to apply the answers the teacher's one way was difficult for me. I could not truly show what I had learned, and I often made mistakes, lost points, or received lower grades as a result. It wasn't that I *didn't know* the content; I just *didn't know how* to make it fit into the worksheet.

Why Choices Matter

Looking back now, I believe that if I had been given more of a choice, my grades and focus might have been better in my classes, especially those which I found to be challenging. But instead, because I tried to learn by essentially memorizing answers to worksheet questions in preparation for the test, little of that early knowledge stayed with me. I practiced for the unit tests by studying the answers to questions from quizzes or worksheets. I was not really good at transferring my knowledge, and preparing for class this way was not helping me to develop those skills. As a visual learner, I could remember what the information in the book or my notes "looked like," but I could only respond if the questions were the same as on the practice worksheet. For a long time, I was unable to transfer and apply knowledge to different contexts.

To help, my parents made sure that I was prepared for more than answering those scripted questions. The routine was that my parents would give me time to study and then one of them would "quiz me" to see if I had prepared enough. There was one catch. I had to get most of the questions, if not all of them, right. I would read the book and review my papers, but I would still miss a bunch of geography questions when my mom or dad quizzed me. But why, especially when I had done the work and reviewed my notes from class? Because I was still preparing by learning the answers to the questions that were already asked, not by making my own questions or thinking through how I could apply my knowledge to other scenarios. This proved problematic for a few reasons. More important to me at the time, if I did not answer enough questions correctly, I would not be watching any TV shows that night. As a 1980s kid, before the invention of VCRs, DVRs, or the arrival of Netflix, if I missed a show, there wasn't much hope in catching it in a rerun or recording it onto a videotape. So, the pressure was on. I had to get the questions right.

But things in education were different back then compared to now. Less emphasis was placed on choices in learning. It was more traditional and somewhat rigid unless the teacher decided to take some risks with their instructional methods in the classroom. Not that there's anything wrong with "traditional," although I think it is vitally important to change and evolve our practice. I feel pretty comfortable saying and thinking that most educators out there today have changed from teaching the way that they had been taught, perhaps because methods are outdated, or they simply have new ideas and new ways to connect students with the content.

There is nothing wrong with the older, traditional methods if that is what works best for the students. So, I guess when my parents asked me questions, they were thinking about what's best for *this learner*, and I was *that learner*. I can clearly recognize this now, but my seventh-, eighth-, and ninth-grade self did not see this as clearly back then. Years ago, as a law school student, I wished for that same parental support in preparing for my exams, because it really worked. But it was time for me to do it on my own, and because of how my parents helped me to prepare when I was younger, I was able to find my way.

CHALLENGE: SHARE A CHANGE YOU MADE THAT LED TO A SIGNIFICANT IMPACT ON STUDENTS OR SHARE YOUR FAVORITE QUOTE.

#QUOTES4EDU

MY FRIENDSHIP WITH AMY

I've known Amy for a few years, having met her through Twitter and being an ambassador in some of the same ambassador programs. We became friends simply by connecting through the power of social media, especially Voxer and I have learned so much from her. We are connected in the #4OCFPLN and learn from one another each day. One thing that is obvious, even in the first moments of hearing Amy talk, is her passion for and love of teaching and students.

Chapter 3

LOVE FIRST. TEACH SECOND

BY AMY STORER - FOR JED AND BRAEDEN

Heart before mind,
Pedagogy before technology,
Process before product.

The first time that I ever got the chance to meet Jed Dearybury, I just knew that he was going to be someone who would inspire me often and push me to be the best educator that I could be. We met a few years ago through a mutual friend, Julie Jones, and when he shared this quote with me, it caused a ripple of energy within my soul. That's all it took. Four words.

Love first. Teach second.

What does this truly mean? It means that we must reach the heart before we can ever reach the mind. But I also think that it means that we have to love the job we've been blessed with and with that comes being solid in our pedagogy — in knowing that you will get more from your kids through conversation, collaboration, and creation than any other cookie cutter worksheet or boxed curriculum that you can purchase online. That word "love" in Jed's quote means so much more than meets the eye. It means loving ourselves, loving our students, loving our campus home, and loving what we do. When these things happen, the teaching will follow with such a force that your *kids will want to learn, not have to learn*.

This quote doesn't just belong within the four walls of our class-rooms. It belongs in your campus, district office, the curriculum department, transportation and custodial departments, technology department, and every corner of your district that shapes and molds our students into becoming the wonderful human beings they were destined to be.

When I was in the classroom, I created a sign with this quote that hung on my wall. I wanted my students to know, not only in my actions, but in my heart that this was my classroom pledge to them. When I became an instructional coach, I added this quote to a lightbox that was displayed in my window. I wanted my teachers to know that this was also my pledge to them. Before becoming an instructional coach, I never thought about how these four words applied to everyone who has a stake in our students' futures. This notion of loving and nurturing those in our care doesn't just apply to the classroom. It applies to our school buildings and beyond.

I learned a very tough lesson my first year as an instructional coach. I learned that this job wasn't about me. It was about those that were under my care. It was about their growth and their journey as educators. In an article written for *Education Week,* Peter Dewitt said "[Coaches] help us see our blind spots, and can help bring our instructional practices up to a new level" (Dewitt, 2014). For this to happen, loving them first and teaching them second was an important part of our relationships. But with this also comes a very fine line, and it has taken me almost three years as a coach to understand it. Jim Knight said it best when he said, "Coaches need to affirm the people they coach, but also be careful not to affirm them away from confronting reality. If my positive comments make it easier for you to avoid reality, I'm likely doing it, so you'll think well of me, not because it helps you" (Knight, 2018).

The relationships that I have with those that I work alongside are just one of the many stepping stones of an instructional coach. That is where it all starts, just like it applies to the classroom. But I also have an essential role as a coach to empower and inspire those around me to be their very best so they can be their very best for their students. Being the best for our kids starts with the heart. I feel very strongly about this. Most of the students that will enter our classrooms did not have the same childhood as us. We must be sympathetic and empathetic to that. Every decision that a student makes in the classroom, whether it's positive or negative, can almost always be tied back to their lives and experiences. We must recognize this and do all that we can to help them reach their full potential. We do this by forming stable relationships and being solid in pedagogy. These two are not separate from one another. Our kids deserve our very best, in heart and mind. We have to be passionate about what we are teaching and how it connects to our students. Those connections are crucial. If the students don't care about what they are learning, it honestly won't matter to them. Find ways to make those connections. I can promise you, that they will not make those crucial connections through worksheets, homework, or compliant practices.

Loving our students and appreciating their backgrounds is a must, but we must love them **AND** teach them. Our job, our calling, is to love our kids and to give them the education that they deserve. We can love them all day long, but if our instructional delivery methods are shallow and low-level, our kids will suffer. I have been a witness to great teachers delivering low-level instruction because that is what they were comfortable with. How is that fair to our students? Comfort levels are meant to be challenged and broken. Model that for your students and show them that taking risks and embracing failure is more about the process than the product. Our comfort level is not what our kids need or deserve.

That One Kid

We all have that one kid. You know the one that I am talking about. The kid that challenged us in ways that made us better educators. The kid that schooled us on school. That one kid for me was Braeden. The first day that I met him, these were his exact words. "We are all just robots in this system." I remember looking at him, wide-eyed, and thinking, "He's going to be fun."

This is a sketch that Braeden drew while we were working on forms of energy.

Little did I know that he was going to be the tipping point in my career as an educator. He was going to show me more than I could have ever learned in a four-year educator prep program, in college textbooks and even through online research. The first part of the school year was challenging. I will own the fact that I did not start with the heart with him. I viewed some of his choices in class as defiant, without ever really understanding where he was coming from. Because of this, it took almost half of the school year to form a solid relationship with him. The order in which we do things as educators is essential. **Heart before mind, pedagogy before technology, process before product.** The list could go on and on. I failed him that first semester. But that tipping point that I referred to earlier was just around the corner.

I was lucky to be on a campus where my decision in not assigning homework was approved and encouraged by my campus leader. The only reason that I gave homework before that year was because "that's the way it's always been done." I figured out pretty quickly that this was not a strong enough excuse to assign pages of homework to my students. I have a dear friend, Kristin Sissom, who once told me, "Our students should be leaving school each day

exhausted because we have stretched their learning so much."
When my kids get home, I want them to truly be present at home.
Homework is such a barrier to that. What we are doing in our
classes every day must be intentional and meaningful and with an
absolute sense of urgency. I see the error in this now, but during our
second semester of school, I started something called "Experiences"
(fancy word for homework) for my kids to work on during the
week. I did this because I knew what was coming for them next
year. I knew that their teachers were going to assign them pages of
homework each night, and I didn't want them not to be prepared. I
made a lot of mistakes when I did this, but as with any bump in the
road or struggle, I owned them and learned from them. The decisions that I made that year should have been based on my kids'
needs, not what the following year was going to expect of them.
That was something that I couldn't control, but what I could control
were the decisions and actions that I made for my kids. Let's get
back to that tipping point.

During one of these experiences, I asked my students to solve three
problems involving simplifying fractions. My students knew that
how they decided to show their work and their learning was up to
them, so some of the kids submitted images of their work on paper
via Edmodo, some shared voice recordings, and one boy decided to
be brave and ask a question hoping that I would **just say yes**.
Braeden approached me that week and asked if he could explain
how to simplify fractions by using Minecraft and a screencasting
tool. At the time, I knew very little about Minecraft, but I knew
how important this was to him. Up until then, he challenged me (in
a good way) on turning in a great deal of his work and assignments
in class. I said yes. What came from that simple answer to him was
my and our tipping point. Even his mother could not believe the
effort and time he was putting into making this video the best it
could be. Because, here is the thing: this was a connection for him.
He loved gaming and loved virtual reality, and he wanted to use
those passions to explain how to simplify fractions. When he

approached me with his video, he asked if he could show it to me in private. As soon as I pressed play, I was immersed in hearing him, his voice, talking through his thought processes.

At one point, my eyes filled with tears. This child blew me away. He used pressure plates in Minecraft and a screencast tool to completely walk me through how to simplify fractions. I got more from that video than I could have ever gotten from a worksheet or paper and pencil. He explained to me, in his own words, how to solve the problems. It meant something to him, so it meant something to me. That feeling is so reciprocal in the relationships with our students. When it means something to us, it means something to others and vice versa. Braeden, thank you. Thank you for giving me the tipping point to not only grow more as an educator but to also strengthen our relationship. I will root for you, in life, always!

Love first. Teach second. These four words mean so much more than the room they take up on a page. Don't forget to love yourself, love your students, love your work, and love your journey. Love it all, because what we do as educators is essential work.

Love, and then teach. Love is where it all starts. It all starts with the heart.

Amy Storer is an instructional coach and lead technology integration mentor in Montgomery, TX. She loves being an instructional coach and working alongside the wonderful educators of Keenan Elementary School and Montgomery ISD. She is a distinguished educator that encourages and motivates others to reach far beyond the classroom walls to make learning more meaningful and inspiring. She has a real passion for working with other educators and students to empower them to build and foster global connections.

Chapter 4

THE WAY WE LEARN —
COMPETITION, MISTAKES,
AND CHALLENGES

"You are in competition with no one but yourself." — Unknown

So many times, I tried to compare my own progress and grades with those of my classmates and my friends. My habit of telling my parents that "everyone in the class did bad" or "I got one of the higher grades" (even if it was a C) was a way to protect myself from getting in trouble for receiving lower grades and partially because it helped me to deal with not doing as well. I think it's kind of human nature to make excuses. At least for me, it is something that I have done since childhood. I am more aware of

it now because I had some experiences where excuses, no matter
how good, did not work.

Many times, in defense of not knowing the answer to the test questions, I would say, "Well, Mr. or Mrs. So-and-So didn't give us that
question," or "We didn't have to know that, it wasn't on the
worksheet."

My parents did not want to hear these "excuses" as their response
was always, "It doesn't matter what's on the paper; you need to
know all material. You have to anticipate different questions." My
parents were right, and I kept their advice in my mind, and it
helped me to better prepare and continue to improve the older I
got. Instilling in me that I should worry about myself and what was
best for *me*, the learner, and think beyond the worksheet or the
questions in the book helped me tremendously throughout my life
and in my other educational experiences. It has even positively
impacted my teaching practice today because I can look back and
reflect on my own experiences with learning — especially when it
comes to preparing class materials for my own students.

For many years, I had been creating assessments by using questions
from the worksheets that I created, but not offering different
options for students to apply their knowledge. This was something
I realized a few years into my teaching career. It didn't help me
when I first started teaching because I was unsure of the best
methods and lacked a sufficient background in methodology, so I
went with what I knew and what mostly worked for me: homework, worksheets, drills, tests. Repeat.

Failing my Students

I taught my students how I had been taught when I learned a
foreign language. I avoided methods which I did not like as a
student and made my own decisions based on what worked for
me, and what I "learned" from my own teachers. Looking back

five, 10, 15, or 20 years in my career, I've made a lot of changes — changes which should have been made sooner. And so, I ask you to think about what's best for each learner in your classroom. Don't prepare the lesson for the "class." Don't think about how much you can cover with the class in that confined class period time, between the ringing of the bells. Prepare the lesson for each student by anticipating different questions or different ideas and offer students more choices for how to practice with content. Be flexible if you are not making it through *your* entire plan for the day. Take a risk and be okay with and open to students coming up with their own ideas. Create a space where students feel comfortable telling you that a particular method just isn't working for them. Do this by being present. Ask students for ideas and help with making decisions in the classroom. Show them that they matter, that their opinions matter.

"If a child can't learn the way we teach, maybe we should teach the way they learn." — Ignacio Estrada

---

Have you ever had a student tell you that an assignment is too hard, and they want to give up, only for your response to be maybe they "weren't trying enough," they should "give it one more go," or "figure it out on their own?" Did you help, or blame a lack of effort rather than a lack of instructional planning or providing alternate materials and accommodations? Meaning, did you accept that you needed to do more?

It's okay to admit mistakes, and I have been admitting mistakes over the past few years, a lot of them! Maya Angelou said, "We do the best we can until we know better and when we know better, we do better." I'm sure many of us think that we were doing right by our students, but perhaps now you may have some doubts, and that's okay because we're all learners and it's an ongoing process.

We try, we fail, we learn and improve as we go. The key is not to stop, even when we feel like we just can't do it or feel like asking for help is a sign of weakness. It is not. We are all learners and must do what is best for us so we can do what's best for those we lead. Getting help might mean shadowing a teacher, enrolling in a course, or asking an administrator to come in and observe us, or something even scarier: asking students for feedback. Students are directly impacted by our methods, our actions, our attitudes, and we owe it to them to be receptive to their feedback. They might be brutally honest, or not be the best at sugar coating their feedback, but they need to be part of the conversation. John Hattie found that 95% of what teachers do to enhance student achievement works. To continue to do what's best for students, it is vital that we invite their feedback and use it to design the best possible learning experiences and classroom culture for them. Start a conversation. Ask students to share their ideas; show them that they are valued in the classroom and in making some classroom decisions.

Learn with and From Me, Grow with Me

Think about some students you've had over the years who either quickly finished a class worksheet or task and then waited around for the other students to finish. Or the student who worked tediously on the assignment, took it home to complete, only to return the next day with it incomplete because they did not understand what they were supposed to do. Likely there was no way for them to ask questions beyond the school day. For these students, learning stops, frustration can set in, walls go up, and the perception of school and learning becomes negative.

As educators, what should we do in these situations? How can we provide for each student, so they are engaged in learning and have the support they need whenever they need it? Possibilities to consider: Do you give extra work to the student who finishes on time? Do you give less work to the student who needs more time, so that they can finish? It is not an easy answer. All students need to have the same access to learning, but it's okay if it comes in different forms at different times. We must meet the needs of every learner in the classroom and figuring out the best way to do this takes time.

Jon Craig
Instructional Coach
Harry S Truman High School
Bristol Township School District
@coachjoncraig

"In any moment of decision, the best thing you can do is the right thing, the next best thing is the wrong thing, and the worst thing you can do is nothing." - Theodore Roosevelt

We live in a rapidly evolving world as educators, where the newest technologies, standards, research studies, and more are brought before us at a seemingly, unprecedented rates. When combined with administrative, political, and community pressures, these tasks can feel impossible, so an easy option for teachers can be to shut the classroom door and continue to run the classroom the way it's always been done. However, if we do not look to update our practice, if we do not take risks, if we do not try to use the available data and research to inform our decisions, how can we expect our students to do the same? We must model the learning process we want our students to adopt.

Sometimes we'll do the right thing and cultivate an amazing experience. Unfortunately, at times, we'll do the wrong thing and not meet our desired outcomes. In those moments, our students are watching to see how we handle it, which provides a great opportunity to demonstrate the struggle of a learning process. Both of those situations can produce desirable results which have a positive impact on kids. However, we all could agree that no changes and no risks, at best, can only produce the same results, with no growth. Let's bet on our own abilities as educators and take those risks. It won't be the worst thing you could do.

NOTHING CAN SUBSTITUTE EXPERIENCE
— PAOLO COELHO

"Be brave. Take risks. Nothing can substitute experience."

— *Paolo Coelho*

Sometimes you must think creatively and involve students to find out what works best for them. Forget about the worksheets, packets, and text activities, and break away from what has been your traditional way of doing things in class, because it may not be working. Instead, be flexible in planning and welcoming new ideas. Maybe pair students up, to enable the student who needs extra help to learn with a peer and build their skills together. For the student who finishes early, perhaps they can apply their knowledge in a way that is beneficial to their peers, such as helping to facilitate the lesson. By having students work together, it not only builds their knowledge in the content area, but it also fosters critical skills that they will need for the future beyond the walls of your classroom or school. The benefits are equally as great for the educator, who can then use the extra time to move around the classroom, interact with each group, engage in the conversations happening, and observe the learning that is taking place in different and unique ways for each group of students. The best part is that as educators, we learn new methods from our students. We see how they learn best and can add it to our practice. They help to keep us relevant in our methods.

We may stand at the front, and we may have studied for many years while preparing to enter the teaching profession, but we never stop learning. We cannot. Our learning is not limited to what is provided by a specific professional organization, in training done within our school or from attendance at a conference. Learning is everywhere and happens every day. Students can teach us a lot about teaching. We are all learners and all leaders, and everyone has something to offer.

"If you're not prepared to be wrong, you'll never come up with anything original." — *Sir Ken Robinson*

Kristi Daws
Technology Integration Specialist
Region 9 Education Service Center
@kristi_daws

This was me in 1997 when I began my teaching career. I was so anxious to please everyone. I wanted to know exactly what they needed so I could quickly complete all tasks and make them happy...

...and I did. I made everyone happy.

I saw so many things going on in education that I thought could be better — so many things that would improve the classroom experience for my students. The problem is: I kept doing the same activities and assessments in my middle school math class. Maybe you are familiar with this process. The students enter the classroom. We exchange papers and grade. I show them the notes on the board for the next unit. I model some problems. We work through some problems. Now it is their turn to do problems as they sit working quietly at their desks. I move around the room until the bell rings, and what they have not completed is now homework.

Yes, I did that.

It took me a while to wrap my head around it, but if I wanted change, it had to start with me. It wasn't easy. My colleagues (and some parents) were confused that I changed my classroom formula. My answer to them was always, "Just give it a chance and see what happens."

What I immediately noticed was not only could I smile before Christmas, but I could laugh and talk with my students about things other than Math. Relationships started to build.

I did not need to "grade" everything we did. In fact, if the students knew that it wasn't going to "count against them" they were willing to try crazy things along with me. We could make mistakes, reflect, adjust, and learn together. I moved easily into cooperative learning, flexible seating, student voice, and placing relationships above all.

I started reading books about education (I know I should have done it much earlier), blogs, followed Twitter chats, and built my own PLN. Along the way, I discovered that I was not the only one who thought like this.

I wish I could go back and apologize to all the students I worked with at the beginning of my career. I could have done better. I wasn't prepared to be wrong. I am now. In fact, I am proud to say that I am wrong often. It is okay as long as you learn and grow from that.

———

We are learners. There will be moments when we realize that we did not make the best or right decision, that we failed, and that it had a negative impact on our students and ourselves. Like Kristi, I had that same practice in my own classroom for years — until I realized that it was not working. As educators, we have difficult decisions to make in the work that we do, and we must be willing to step in and do what is right, not what is easy. Everything in life prepares us for something. It might mean we have to experience something that's difficult or goes against what others *expect* us to do, but we are presented with challenges in life that are unique to each one of us. Our skills, our fears, our passions, and our purpose are in some way connected to these challenges. Every single experience is preparation for something; we just don't know what for or when we might need it. Take advantage of every opportunity to conquer fears, to embrace failures, and to build resilience. It is in those moments where we might feel the most helpless or weak that we have the most strength.

Be the one who makes a difference, who stands up to fight, to DARE (Dream, Advocate, Risk, Empower), and do what you believe in. And when you feel the struggle or question yourself, remember that you have overcome many other challenges and bumps before. The key is to be true to yourself and stay connected to your why.

"One of the most courageous things you can do is identify yourself, know who you are, what you believe in and where you want to go."
– Sheila Murray Bethel

Dr. Toutoule Ntoya
Instructional Coach
Pasadena, CA
@toutoulentoya

Doing what's right: Believing in students.

I was on the teaching staff, and we were making decisions about the first set of AP classes and which students would be in the class. There were some folks on the staff, and it was a small staff, and some who thought that the AP process should be very exclusive. They wanted the kids who could "handle it," who had the perceived cognitive ability. I stepped into one of the meetings, and I said, "Listen, this AP class. With the student population we have, we should not be exclusive. It should be open. We should find a way to open it up to the general population and allow kids to join if they want." It's our job as teachers to push them if they want it.

Well, there was some back-and-forth talk about kids who couldn't handle it, whose reading levels were low, attention spans were low, and so much more. So, I pretty much laid a line in the sand and said, "Listen, this is how it has to be." I wasn't teaching the class. Somebody else was, but I put my two cents in and said it's not fair. Honestly, I wish I would have had the mindset that I have now and transport myself back to that conversation because I would have said we need to give our kids the opportunity. But thinking about it and everything that I've learned in all my experiences now, the real conversation should have been that we were teaching a population of historically marginalized students, and we can't continue to marginalize those students by making this opportunity exclusive.

We came to a consensus, and it was kind of a trade-off that kids would go through an application process. It was open for anyone to apply, but it was still up to the teacher whether the student could enter. That was so problematic for me because we became gatekeepers of a class, especially for a class that could be very instrumental in helping students get into college. So that was the compromise, and when I talked to the students about the situation, I said if you think you can take this AP class, then take it. And if you think that you may not be up for the class, take it anyways. Because you'll never know what you can or can't do until you actually get in the mix of doing it.

So, what is the lesson for us? We want students to take risks with learning in our classrooms. We expect them to try and be okay with not knowing the answer or making a mistake. We encourage them to not give up by supporting them along the way. We need to do the same for ourselves. Give ourselves grace for not always having the answer. Allow ourselves to take risks, be different and learn from our own failures.

"There is no innovation and creativity without failure. Period."

— Brené Brown

CHALLENGE: THINK ABOUT YOUR TEACHING STYLE; DO YOU TAKE RISKS, ARE YOU OPEN TO FAILURE? SHARE AN EXPERIENCE AND LESSON LEARNED. TAG A MEMBER OF YOUR PLN WHO IS ALWAYS THERE TO SUPPORT YOU.

#QUOTES4EDU

MY FRIENDSHIP WITH MELISSA

I met Melissa through the #games4ed chat on Twitter and finally got to meet her in person at the Summer Spark conference in June of 2018. It is amazing how you can feel like you've known someone for so long, even when meeting face-to-face for the first time. My understanding of game-based learning and gamification has increased, and more than that, I have been inspired by Melissa's positivity and her constant passion for education.

Chapter 5

LESSONS FROM MY WORST
YEAR OF TEACHING

MELISSA PILAKOWSKI

"Bad times have a scientific value. These are occasions a good learner would not miss." — *Ralph Waldo Emerson*

L et me tell you about my worst year of teaching.

It wasn't my first. It was my tenth — a decade into my career when I thought I had this teaching gig figured out.

Nothing could be further from the truth.

My family had moved four hours from my previous district, so I applied for a position in our new district (which, ironically, was the one where I had done my student teaching). When the principal offered me the job, he warned me that the incoming sophomores that I'd be teaching were a class "that needed a lot of love," and that they had been notorious as "that class" ever since kindergarten. *No problem*, I'd thought. I had experience with challenging kids. My classroom management was so solid, my rapport with students so good, that I would be fine.

At the end of day one, I was beyond exhausted. By the end of the first month, I didn't know how I would survive the school year. So many students wouldn't listen to me. They wanted to poke fun at each other, yell at each other across the room, do anything other than the assignment that I'd given. I learned to dismiss students from class one row at a time because having an entire class up and moving led to piggyback rides and wrestling matches. Limiting student movement went against everything I believed, but tracking a handful of students moving at one time was definitely easier than tracking 20 of them.

All of my creative lessons that had been successful in the past proved impossible. Group activities quickly disintegrated into off-task conversations. I'd warn them, again and again, to get back on task. I'd threaten them with office referrals. I'd keep them after school. Not only did this not work, but it seemed to fuel them to continue their misbehavior. I'd consulted my principal and other teachers, but they were just as exhausted with this group as I was.

Then, there was the guilt for the students who were trying to learn. So much of my time was spent trying to control the off-task students that I spent precious little of my attention on the students wanting to learn and staying on-task. They didn't complain much — likely because they were used to these classmates since they'd gone to school with them since kindergarten — but guilt weighed on me when I looked at them. They tried to be patient, but I could tell they'd given up on my ability to stop this three-ring circus.

Trying to Make it Through

Eventually, against my belief of "good teaching," I returned to worksheets and packets so that I could survive the year. As it turned out, this was what other teachers had been doing too. "It just seems like that's what they want," the teacher across the hall from me confided. "Give them a worksheet, and that's the only time they're quiet and happy." The packets did keep them quiet. I'm sure for the students who were trying to learn, the packets were a blessing. For the other students — well, for whatever reason, they also behaved best with a packet in front of them. On those days, I drove home thinking maybe I could do this, even though my conscience still nagged at me, telling me that these worksheets were nothing but busy work — the purest example of busy work. Students may have been learning, but the purpose of the packets was to keep them quiet and under control.

Eventually, the end of the school year arrived, and my principal pulled me in and gave me some news: I'd be teaching some of these students again as juniors. After progressing through shock, denial, and finally acceptance, I decided to alter my approach. I couldn't go in trying to control the pace of the class. I would move at their pace, and if we didn't get done with what I thought we should during that class period, we'd just carry it over to the next day. I didn't push homework on them, knowing it would never be done. These small changes seemed to click. My students focused more on our classwork, and I didn't have the same distractions and rough-housing from the year before. Best of all, no more office referrals or detentions. The few times that I did have a problem with a student, I pulled them aside or into the hallway — much easier to do when the rest of the class is on task — and the student and I would have that conversation in private. No longer being the center of attention, the students responded much better and effectively than calling them out in front of their classmates.

I also worked in more of their interests. I surveyed their careers and applied our lessons and assignments to those careers, giving examples of how a cattle rancher or welder or cosmetologist would use that lesson in the future. I tapped into pop culture by using examples of Eminem lyrics for teaching idioms or analyzing the movie Ocean's Eleven when we studied group communication. Following these lessons, students would voluntarily bring in examples from other songs or films! In the end, I actually enjoyed the class. They had grown up, and so had I. I've celebrated their college graduations, attended their weddings (two of them to each other), and even held their babies.

The moral of this story could focus on courage and perseverance during the rough years, which is true. There will always be rough years. But there will be amazing years, too.

What's more important is how this challenging, frustrating group of students sparked a transformation in my teaching and led me to embark on the route of moving to a student-led classroom. It all started when I'd heard that other teachers had resorted to handing out worksheets or packets to keep the class under control. I was relieved, but it also bothered me. This wasn't how learning was supposed to be. Was this "old-school" method of school really the only answer for years when we faced challenging students? I started thinking about what could have made the year more successful. Had I started the year with too many activities that they didn't see as worthwhile? How well had I gotten to know them and their personalities in the first few weeks of school?

I also worried about my classroom management. What did it say about me that I struggled so much with these students? This also shook one of my beliefs that I'd touted in my job interview: classroom discipline is a moot point when lessons are effective, and students are engaged. Why didn't my engaging lessons from the past fall flat this year?

My second year at the school, when I relaxed more with the students, they responded to me better. I'd spend the first few minutes of class chatting with them — about life, current events, or whatever was on their minds. I didn't need to rush into the lesson. I paid attention to their energy levels and moods, and I adjusted my lessons to them.

When the senior English teacher retired, I took over her classes, and with that came devices for a 1:1 classroom. Immediately, I saw the power of using technology to allow students to work at their own pace and timing. I spent more time working with students and less time leading lessons at the front of the room. I felt more connected to each student by chatting with them one-on-one almost every day, Students would still get off-task, but they were less distracting to other students, who were immersed in their work, and this let me chat with the "off-taskers" and find out what was going through their minds. Maybe I wasn't always successful getting them back on task that day, but over time when I continued this approach, they spent less time off-task and more time focused on our classwork. Eventually, my number of office referrals became non-existent.

Soon, I immersed myself in the world of Twitter, where I learned from scores of educators more experienced than I. At first, I only browsed my Twitter stream, but then I started participating in Twitter chats and learning how they worked. A few months later, I crossed virtual paths with Steve Isaacs and Dr. Matt Farber, and together we started the #games4ed Twitter chat. These two served as my mentors in the fields of gamification and game-based learning. These Twitter chats connected me to many other gamified teachers, but more importantly, they also connected me to expert teachers in other areas of education. Our conversations in Twitter chats made me rethink my purposes for assessments and worksheets and dead-end assignments. They gave me the courage to include more student choice by providing two or three different options for an assignment. That led to different choices for independent reading projects. Soon I was providing some type of student choice on almost every assignment or project.

I didn't know it at the time, but my classroom was morphing from a teacher-led class to a student-led one.

This is how my classroom is different today, all thanks to my worst year of teaching. Ever.

Nearly all the work that we do is accessible to students 24/7. Students can access our daily agendas at any time and know exactly what they need to do. They can move at their own pace (within reason — we still have deadlines) and use multiple resources (such as interactive readings and videos) to learn.

I meet with students at the end of units to review what they learned and help them to set new goals. They tell me where they want to improve. And together, we come to a consensus about a grade for that unit.

I limit the amount of time I teach a lesson to 5-10 minutes. Sometimes I even have a student time me if I can sense that students are unsettled; this serves as a guarantee that I will only take up that time and then they can have work time.

I spend more time working with students in small groups or one-on-one. With one student, I might reinforce what a thesis is and how to strengthen theirs, while I might teach a more advanced student how to create flow quotes in their writing. Not all students are learning the same things, but they're learning what they need at that moment.

We still have some whole-class activities, such as peer review days for essays, but I limit them to 1-2 days a week.

I give students choices based on what the learning objective is. If the objective is based on a skill, such as writing an argument, then students get a choice in the topic. If the objective is based on content, such as Macbeth, students choose how they want to learn. They may read the text online, where they can read it without assistance, or can have the text read to them via online tools, or can watch the play while they read. They also have choices in how they demonstrate their learning. Some students struggle when given a wide range of options, so I do provide some possibilities or examples of student work from the past; however, I always leave students the option to create their own plan or topic for a paper or project.

Students choose where they sit in the room. Some tables and chairs are set up for those who like to work with groups; other tables and chairs are against the wall for students who need few distractions. Other students choose to sit on the couch, the moon chairs, or pillows on the floor.

What if?

I think back on my worst year of teaching. If this group walked into my classroom today, how would they react? Could we all be more successful and happier in a student-led class?

I'll be honest — it would take time to release more choices and freedom to them. They would need to learn the norms and mores of a student-led classroom. The process might be slow until they trusted me and knew that I would honor their choices and interests.

I wish I could have that year back and give those students another shot. I'd given them more options and choices in their learning. I'd spend less time leading a class through step-by-step lectures and more time working with them individually. Most of all, I'd prioritize relationships from the beginning and ask them how and what they like to learn. Building relationships is the one thing I emphasize with new teachers who enter our building. Take your time in those first weeks getting to know your students through surveys and conversations, doing teamwork activities such as the Marshmallow Challenge, and celebrating their successes. Build your classroom culture first, and if you do that, they'll be much more ready to learn the content.

MELISSA PILAKOWSKI IS an 11-12 ELA teacher from Valentine, Nebraska. An advocate of playful and gameful learning, she's always on the lookout for a new twist to bring fun and engagement to her students' learning. She's also interested in everything related to literacy, technology, and student metacognition. Join her and the #games4edcrew on Thursday evenings, follow her on Twitter @mpilakow or check out her blog at technologypursuit.edublogs.org.

Chapter 6

FINDING OUR PASSION AND PURPOSE

The one thing that you
have that nobody else has is you.
Your voice, your mind
your story, your vision
So write and draw and build
and play and dance and live
as only you can. — Neil
Gaiman

Tisha Richmond

"The one thing that you have that nobody else has is you. Your voice, your mind, your story, your vision. So, write and draw and build and play and dance and live as only you can. "

— *Neil Gaiman, Author*

Have you ever wondered what your true purpose is? Like even though you've been doing something for your whole life, whether working the same job or participating in an activity, or maybe avoiding something because of fear, you wonder if there's more out there. As a student, I wondered why I needed to learn certain skills, ones which I "knew" (or at least thought) I would never use. As a teacher, I catch myself thinking the same thing for my students — wondering about their future and whether it will involve the content that I have taught them, or if I have missed opportunities to make a more significant impact in their lives.

For years, I was content-focused. Students had to memorize vocabulary and verbs specific to certain themes, grammatical constructions, cultural facts, and whatever the *book* provided. I missed opportunities to share personal experiences or to make connections with students beyond the class period. I followed my plan and hesitated for years to break that thinking and those teaching habits. It was comfortable, but it was not fostering student inquiry and sparking curiosity. Learning in a sense was finite. Beyond my own purpose for knowing foreign languages, I didn't do much to encourage students to connect with the content in their own ways, based on their interests. Knowing that a student loves sports, plays an instrument, or wants to travel would make a difference in how they connect with the content and within our classroom. It would engage them in more authentic learning that matters.

"You can teach a student a lesson for a day; but if you can teach him to learn by creating curiosity, he will continue the learning process as long as he lives." — Clay P. Bedford

---

Jeff Kubiak
Elementary School Principal
California
@jeffreykubiak

Growing up, I was fortunate to have parents who allowed my sister and me to partake in as many activities as possible. While some may have only lasted a short time (piano, karate, and flag football to name a few), just having the exposure and experience was a gift.

Because of these amazing opportunities, I have since become a lifelong swimmer, skier, scuba diver, snorkeler, camper, water enthusiast, and so much more all because I had the chance to tease my curiosity with a wide array of activities.

Although some of my experiences were short-lived (one time, sorry mom), I was given lessons and instruction, that to this day, 45 +/- years later, I still remember. My curiosity was piqued. My love of learning was enhanced. My will to excel in certain things grew, and I continue the learning process even now.

I began swimming competitively at the age of four. Over the years, there were many peaks and valleys (such as missing the Olympic Swim Team in '88 by .12), and my love for the sport either grew or was diminished based on each coach or instructor I had. It's been almost 50 years since then, and I am still a lover of the sport.

Why? Well, my parents' goal was always to keep me as busy as possible. Thanks to Mom and Dad, as well as having wonderful coaches, amazing experiences, and making life-long friendships along the way, my curiosity has led me to the pursuit of learning every day since.

Mr. Bedford's quote correlates so beautifully to education. My experiences in school as a youngster were not all happy — some were even horrible (fifth grade, having my head slammed against the wall outside the classroom by my teacher…). But you throw in a fantastic teacher like Mrs. Sherry in sixth grade at West Davis Elementary School and *boom!* You now have someone who sparked curiosity, kept me engaged in lessons, and inspired my love of learning.

So, I leave you with this to marinate on — expose and introduce our youth to as many activities, subjects, modalities, and ideas as possible. Dangle the carrot. Ignite the curiosity for them to want to learn, for them to need to learn. These opportunities may inspire them not only to become lifelong learners but also lovers of learning.

———

JEFF'S STORY likely resonates with each of us. Think of a teacher like Mrs. Sherry who had an impact on your life and love of learning. We need to ask ourselves what our real purpose as educators is. Think about our roles in the lives of the students in our classrooms, beyond content delivery. We are the facilitators, the advocates, the mentors, the innovators, the coaches, the parents, and the learners. With all our responsibilities, we must lead by example and be the positives in the lives of our students. By our words and actions, strive to inspire those we lead to build the skills required for future success.

---

*"What we **model** is what we get."* — Jimmy Casas

Did you ever take a moment to stop and look around your classroom to observe the actions and attitudes of the students in your care? I think it's interesting to observe, as a way to gather information about how students are interacting and even take note of the messages they are conveying, whether it's through words, gestures, or body language. Students might be doing the same thing, looking at us for guidance about how to act and what to think about learning. Without us even realizing it, they may follow our lead, whether positive or not, and whether we know it or not. I try to be mindful of my teacher presence in the classroom, the school, and even online. There are days where I am affected by something, whether I did not handle a situation well or I am dealing with a personal issue, yet I do my best to keep composure and stay positive. There have been days where I struggled and honestly wanted to go home, or not teach and instead give students busy work for the class to give myself time to recharge. But I just couldn't. If we want students to push through adversities and to embrace learning and all of its struggles, then we need to model these same traits and characteristics for them. Let's show students when we get knocked down in our own pursuit of learning, when our ideas fail, and how we recover and carry on. It's a vital part of teaching students about embracing failures and growth mindset.

We encourage others to act when we model the behaviors and traits that we are trying to promote. Modeling is so important in the life of an educator. Even when we don't realize it, our actions can turn into words. Our most subtle mannerisms are sending a message or conveying a certain presence about us in the ways through which we relate with one another. Without realizing it, we can leave a lasting impression on those around us. What is the message we are sending?

Would you do what you ask of them?

For many years, I asked students to complete assignments or projects or carry out tasks in class that I likely would not have even wanted to do. It's not that I realized this at the time, but later on, after different experiences, I started to recognize that I had been going about some things in the wrong way. It's not that I necessarily knew better and chose to do it differently; I just had not given myself the time to think about it. I relied on teaching strategies and grading practices that I was accustomed to as a student. Of course, that did not make it right or a good fit for my students.

I remember many times as I handed out papers or assigned tasks, students would put up a fight about what I was asking them to do. They cringed at having to speak in class and present in front of their peers, and I could not understand why. Why would they feel uncomfortable talking in front of their classmates, people who they had spent many days, if not years, with beforehand? After 15 years of teaching, I finally understood. One professional development session and two seventh grade students made the light bulb go on, and I had my answer. I realized that I had been asking students to do something that was so uncomfortable for them, but when in the same situation with my own peers, I avoided it at all costs.

Asking students to present in front of their peers, speak in French or Spanish, perform skits, or simply respond to questions seemed like typical tasks. I had not thought about anything beyond my requirement to have them do these performance-based tasks and assessments in the classroom. I simply continued to assign different projects and had not acknowledged or considered that students might feel uncomfortable. I designed activities that were similar to the way I learned in high school and college French classes or other classes where public speaking and presentations were part of the norm. I can clearly remember many conversations with students who begged and tried to bribe me (with coffee) to let them simply write their information, not to have to stand up in front of their classmates and speak. They offered suggestions for how they could complete the same task, but in a way that didn't involve public speaking. I listened to their ideas. However, I was set on them completing the tasks as I had designed them without room for negotiations because that is how it had always been.

But I remember that morning when those seventh-grade students presented to a room full of teachers, speaking to us about creating book trailers and the impact on learning. You could see their excitement about sharing. What struck me the most was that they didn't seem to have any fear. They were confident and seemed comfortable presenting, and I thought to myself how much I would not want to speak to a room full of educators, even my colleagues. It occurred to me that I had such fear of doing what I had been asking (and even demanding) that my students do. It was something I was not willing to do myself and avoided whenever I could. But seeing these two students present was my wake-up call, and that's when I knew better, so I made it a point to do better.

It Starts with Us

From that point on, I decided to start putting myself out there, work on building my confidence, and do things a little bit differently. I needed to model these behaviors for students and continue to better myself. There's always room for improvement, reflection, and growth, and sometimes it's the students who show us that maybe we're not doing things the best that we could or should. So, when we think about modeling, we should project the qualities and traits that we want for our students, ones that will lead them to success. The more we invest ourselves in projecting collaboration, confidence, relationship building, supporting others, and embracing our differences, students will notice. Hopefully, it will become part of who they are and how they act as well. We know it's easy to misinterpret a facial expression or a gesture in the absence of clear communication and language, so we can make a lot of mistakes in our understanding of others. We need to be clear about what it is that we want to share with our students, besides the content that we are teaching. What do our mannerisms, expressions, and "vibe" tell our students?

As educators, we all have a responsibility to help students develop the critical skills that they will need for their future such as collaboration, communication, creativity, and critical thinking. We need to model proper behaviors when it comes to these four C's. Our interactions and responses to our peers will help us to model effective and positive collaboration and communication. When we invite students and colleagues to give us feedback, to come up with new ideas, to problem-solve, and we show that we value their opinion, we model how to foster and promote creativity and critical thinking. We are all learners in the classroom, and as educators, we do have the edge and a higher level of expectations held up for us. If we want students to see the value in learning, we need to be excited about learning, ourselves. And if we want students to know the value in working through challenges and taking risks, we need to take risks and share our struggles in front of the students, even inviting them to help us work through them as part of our ongoing development.

"Being a professional," Julius Erving once said, "is doing the things you love to do, on the days you don't feel like doing them.'"

Think about some of the educators you know, those you had as a student or colleagues that you have worked with throughout your teaching career. Do you remember (or have you noticed) any negative attitudes toward classes, initiatives, procedures, or student behavioral problems, or anything related to the teaching practice itself? I've had a few teachers that openly complained about student behaviors, grading, the workload, and it made me not want to be in their class. Why should I care about and invest in a class when the teacher does not? Students are very impressionable and perceptive. They can quickly sense a negative attitude toward a class and knowing that the teacher has this feeling, it is going to be kind of difficult to overcome that same feeling themselves.

Think about your colleagues, especially if you spend time in the teachers' lounge eating lunch. If you listen in on the conversations (whether or not you try to), what are teachers talking about? Are they excited for the day, sharing stories of student learning, or is it just a 30-minute period of negative talk, that led you to decide not to spend any time in there because it will bring down your positive spirit?

It does not take long for students to sense it, and like I said, even when you think they're not listening or observing, they are. I can't tell you how many times I've had students come in and ask me questions or share information based on what they saw or "thought" they saw or heard — or maybe indeed did. Modeling positivity and being real is important.

We need to model the value in working hard and place emphasis on the process of learning, rather than the product. If this is what we want for our students and colleagues, then this is what we need to model, so that this is what we get. We need to help students move past thinking about the grades and points, and instead to deeply understand the purpose behind learning and how to transfer and apply that learning to life.

We need to model this ourselves as well. We can't expect students and colleagues to have enthusiasm, spread the positivity, and come in excited for learning if we are not doing the same. It starts with us. The way we make our students feel, the opportunities we provide, the interactions we have, and the lessons that we teach that are not part of the curriculum may end up being a critical moment for a student now or in the future.

What are the lessons you learned from your teachers? How have you developed as an educator because of your own experiences? What moments in your educational career made a difference?

"Everyone who remembers his own education remembers teachers, not methods and techniques. The teacher is the heart of the educational system." — *Sidney Hook*

Zee Ann Poerio
Computer (STREAM) Teacher, K-8
Pittsburgh, PA
@MagistraZee

When I think back to my education, I always recall the TEACHERS who were terrific role models, made learning fun, challenged me, or encouraged me to want to do more — elementary school teachers like Sister Rose Marie who was a model of kindness. She instilled the importance of thinking of others first and always being respectful. We may have lined up to take turns reading sight words on flash cards, or maybe we wrote our spelling words multiple times, but my most vivid memories were wanting to do my best every day and to make her happy.

In middle school, Mrs. Safara had the most beautiful handwriting and was an excellent proofreader. I don't remember how she taught us the rules of grammar, but I always checked my subject-verb agreement, punctuation, and used my very best handwriting before turning in any essay to her. She was an expert. She loved what she was doing, and I wanted her to notice that I listened and learned.

I remember laughing at silly jokes or examples that my high school science teacher, Mr. Erett, would tell to help us remember facts. I remember Ms. Lozosky, my Student Council Advisor and social studies teacher who taught me about leadership. I loved being in Mr. Esno's English classes and having him as the director of our school plays. His encouragement and guidance were my primary motivation for becoming a teacher.

I loved singing in the musicals for Mrs. McAuley and playing the clarinet in Mr. Fechter's marching band. I learned so much from Mr. Yothers in painting class and loved it when he told me that I would win a prize with one of my paintings (I did). I still remember critiques in college art classes with Ms. Maloney and Mr. Edwards, and their recommendations and advice. I will never forget Dr. Taylor's Intro to Art History classes, where I developed a real appreciation for art from all eras. Because of the unique personalities and the connections I had with my own teachers, I wanted to learn as much as I could from them. They were dedicated, they made learning exciting, and showed that they cared. I may not have adopted their teaching styles, but I know I honor them by bringing what I have learned from them into my own classroom.

ZEE BEAUTIFULLY TIES TOGETHER her experiences and what she learned from teachers along her journey as a student. Reading her story and knowing the educator she is today, I can recognize the impact these teachers had on her. What will your students say about you, years from now, long after they have left your classroom and have their own jobs, possibly even as educators? What will they remember when they think back to their school experience? What will come to mind when they think of you, your class, and the kind of teacher that you were for them? That is something that we need to consider as part of our daily reflective practice. What message are we sending our students that goes beyond the content we are teaching, and shows or tells them who we are, why we are there, and how we plan to make a difference in their lives? What skills are we teaching them that we don't even realize, that might become a big part of who they are, like in Zee's experience?

Students want to know where they stand as learners and how they got to that point. They need to be able to count on your support to figure out what they need to change and how to decide where to go next in their learning adventure. We do what's best for them by preparing and being intentional in our practice. When we know our why, we can find our way. Our why is preparing our students for whatever they may face in the future. The way that we do that is by letting them in to know us and by giving them a solid, comfortable, and caring environment to develop in.

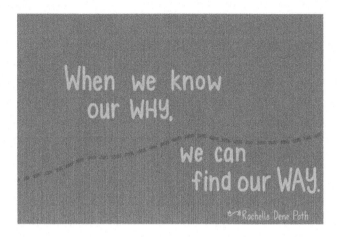

Sarah Fromhold
Digital Learning Coach
Frisco, TX
@sew1080

"Ten, hut!"

Those two tiny words will forever flood my head with memories. Being part of the Coppell High School band under the direction of Mr. Scott Mason taught me many valuable life lessons and forged the trajectory of my future.

Mr. Mason was one of those teachers you heard about long before you became his student. He was tough as nails, expecting nothing but the best from his band members.

Here are some of the lessons I learned from him:

Punctuality: "If you are early, you are on time. If you are on time, you are late." This mantra was ingrained in us from the first day of band camp. I learned to be 15 minutes early to everything, and I am reaping the benefits to this day. Being punctual shows respect. It shows you care about where you are going and the people you will see when you get there.

Organization: Mr. Mason would plan incredibly elaborate trips for his large band down to the minute. Buses needed to pull away from the school at precisely 7:32 a.m. to keep the rest of the day going smoothly. We used to joke about it, but now I realize how beneficial it is to have this trait. Structure and organization were two main components of my class-room, and it helped my students feel safe knowing what was coming next in the day.

Pride: Mr. Mason taught me to do everything with pride. I represented him when I was in class, at football games, or at a competition. Because he garnered such respect, it was important that my actions fostered pride in myself. He passed away in September 2016, after 25 years as the head band director.

Looking at how I live my life today, I grasp what an amazing man he was, and the impact he has had on countless students. Students under his direction, and the lives of students I had in my class. His legacy lives on.

Mistakes happen,
uncertainties exist,
but it's what we do next that defines
us and will become our legacy.

#Quotes4EDU
#Future4EDU

STUDENTS WILL REMEMBER their teachers long after they leave classrooms and schools. Like Sarah, I remember experiences, both positive and negative, that have become a part of who I am as an educator. What do you hope your students will remember about you? I think that's an important consideration to ponder every single day. We must reflect —we must remind ourselves of our real purpose which is doing what's best for students. There will be struggles and many little bumps in the road along the way. There will be times that we may not handle a situation as well as we could have or should have. Mistakes happen, uncertainties exist, but it's what we do next that defines us and will become our legacy. We are in a lifelong learning process; we are *works-in-progress*, working to be better than we were yesterday. Take a few moments to think back to some of your teachers. What are some of the traits that you embody now as a reflection of your own teachers?

CHALLENGE: SHARE YOUR OWN "TEACHER OF IMPACT" STORY AND TAG A MEMBER OF YOUR PLN TO SHARE THEIRS.

#QUOTES4EDU

MY FRIENDSHIP WITH ELIZABETH

I became connected with Elizabeth when we both joined a Voxer book study. You might think it is hard to get to know someone, solely by interacting in a virtual space; however, it is in that space that we became part of a PLN, the #4OCFPLN. In this PLN, we share common passions: a focus on growing, on knowing our why, and on embracing risk-taking. Elizabeth is one of the most passionate educators I know, who fully invests in not only doing what is best for her students but in helping others to do what is best for theirs.

Chapter 7

IT'S WORTH TAKING A RISK

ELIZABETH MERCE

"Be strong enough to stand alone, smart enough to know when you need help, and brave enough to ask it."

– Ziad K. Abdelnour, American Financier and Philanthropist

H ow many of us have worried about whether we were doing what was best for our students? How many of us have compared ourselves with the teacher down the hall who seems to have it all together or even worse, the teacher on social media who is showing the highlight reel?

This comparison to the ideal, whether internally created or from images snatched on social media, can be detrimental to our growth as educators. It can lead to a sense of isolation, fear, anxiety, stress, and unfortunately, it can impact student learning outcomes.

Hattie rates teacher-student relationships as having a .52 effect size (Killian, 2017). Imagine having a strong relationship while feeling stressed, burdened, or burnt out. Not impossible, but difficult. Hattie even says, "When teachers become burned out, or worn out, their student's achievement outcomes are likely to suffer because they are more concerned with their personal survival." (Falecki, 2017).

Abdelnour's quote speaks to a solution that works not only for our own well-being but as a great outline for how to support our learners as they grow. Each part of the quote is important, so I want to address each section separately.

I teach kindergarten. I LOVE it. While I get great joy from teaching my adult learners as well, there is something about kindergarten that is magical. For many littles, it is their first formal experience outside the security of their families. They are being tasked with mastering skills independently. This level of independence is flat out scary for many of our littles. It is eye-opening to see how many of them do not know how to do basic life skills such as blowing their noses, opening packages, going to the restroom, putting on their outerwear, and the list goes on.

This isn't due to some developmental delay. Often it is simply because it is easier, and faster, for the parent to do these tasks for their child. As a mom I get it. As a mom who is often chronologically a single parent to a three-year-old who believes she is a fashionista princess I REALLY get it. As an expert in early learning, I resist the urge to put her shoes on, zip her coat, or even choose her outfits.

Why do I resist? Every time we do something for a child that they can do themselves, we are robbing them of the opportunity to learn and grow. Without scaffolded practice, we cannot expect children to become masters in any skill. When we step in at the first sign of struggle, we are not allowing our learners to figure out how to master skills, and we are robbing ourselves of the chance to learn something new. I cannot count the number of times I've learned how to do something differently because I watched as one of my littles explored a task that was giving them difficulty. Innovation comes from that place of struggle — the place where we examine the parameters of what we know and push into what could be.

How does that look for us as educators? When we stop trying to work things out independently, we are losing out on the ability to push into those innovative spaces. I don't mean to say we shouldn't collaborate or strengthen one another (I'll get to that point later), but merely taking verbatim what others have said or done as the best way to meet the needs of your individual students or yourself is a disservice.

We need to have times where we feel a bit of struggle as we work through things independently. This provides several benefits. One significant advantage is the growth of your self-efficacy as a teacher. You begin to see that you CAN accomplish great things, that your effort and knowledge impacts the growth and learning of your little learners. John Hattie references collective teacher efficacy as one of the factors that has a huge impact on student learning outcomes. How do we get to collective efficacy? As with most things it starts with one. It begins with the individual teacher seeing the fruits of their labor. It begins with you believing that you know what to do as a professional, doing it, and then seeing the results.

Innovation can also be a benefit of independent struggle. I am not saying not to collaborate. Follow me on any social media platform for a day, and you will see that I am a huge believer in collaboration. What I am saying is that you need to work independently on sifting through ideas, trying them, truly analyzing your why, your what, your how, and the outcomes. I can mimic exact lessons from "master teachers" in my classroom and have them flop horribly if I am not looking to match the individual needs of my learners, my teaching style, and my mandated classroom components. When I combine the best practice of our field with the individual needs I have to meet, I create innovative methods that work for my learners. We should all be striving for that personalization.

Another benefit of being strong enough to stand alone is learning *how* you learn. This is true for us as educators and even more so for our little learners. When you are faced with a new situation, you must figure out how to navigate through the work of learning. Cultivating the meta-cognitive skills required for efficient learning takes practice. Since I teach some of the littlest, we talk through the learning process audibly. Walk into any kindergarten classroom during shared writing time, and you will see a teacher audibly thinking about the next word to come in a sentence, where to put spaces, and how to end a sentence while phonetically spelling out words. Go into the same classroom during a "number talk" or "math congress," and you will see the same narration of the thought process taking place as you explore number concepts.

These scenarios may sound solely focused on academics, but it is teaching learners to think about what they are doing as they learn. They build the confidence of our learners to know that we are all struggling through new information and there is a process to think through the unknown. This builds up the educator's sense of what takes place in our own minds as we learn too. Frequently teachers were the students who excelled at school. Because the content came easily, we didn't often stop to think about HOW we learned, so when we confront information that challenges our paradigm we can dig into the old ways — the "how it has always been done" ways. Teaching our learners to work through problems independently strengthens our own ability to understand how we think, which leads to our own increased willingness to accept new information. What an amazing profession we have chosen where helping others helps us to be better than yesterday!

Working through things alone is hard. It is scary. Believing you can solve problems independently leads to tremendous growth. It is our job to support learners as they grow in this area through direct instruction, support, and modeling it in our own lives. But what if you try to tackle something and you are just stuck?

"Smart enough to know when you need help."

After spending time learning how you learn, and working within the belief that you are capable, there will be times when you hit a wall — where collaboration, support, and feedback is not just wanted, but needed. As you think more about your learning and begin to feel more confident in attacking problems on your own, you will start to see more clearly where your deficits are. This is not to say you should focus on your weaknesses, but learn to recognize where they are, which will enable you to know when it is time to ask for help.

When we look at this portion through the lens of our learners, it means teaching them to know when to use the unlimited resources now at their fingertips. When we think about the littlest learners, that may mean simply knowing that they need to use the "word wall" while writing. With our older learners, it may mean teaching them to use the Internet or collaborative software to bridge the gap between the known and unknown

My experience and research lie within the realm of early childhood. When I am asked about something for an adolescent, I have to direct people to resources instead of providing answers. This also means that I have a limited clock to begin building up that knowledge base for myself before my little enters the realm of hormones and independence. I don't feel that my lack of knowledge in this developmental stage means I am less of an educator or less of a parent. I simply know that I have a handle on the early years. I am "smart enough" to know I need to seek out others when confronted with other areas.

I have cultivated a strong Professional Learning Network (PLN) that I use when I am not sure about my own views. This has helped immensely. With a varied network of educators at my fingertips, I can check my understanding on a variety of topics. If I find that I don't know as much as I would like or my understanding does not match theirs, I can move to the next part of the Abdelnour quote.

"Brave enough to ask it."

I fully believe there are times when working independently can have amazing benefits (see the beginning of this chapter!). But once you have hit a roadblock where you are no longer being innovative, no longer being productive, it is time to reach out. Even when we know that we don't have all the answers, it can be hard to ask for help. Have you ever thought about that? There are even cultural jokes about men refusing to ask for directions, even if it means driving into the ocean or off a cliff. As I tend to do, I go back to the why. Why do we resist asking for help? Why do we fall into the trap of sticking to independence?

I think it goes back to the idea of comparison we explored at the beginning. When we reach out to others to collaborate or ask for help, we are showing vulnerability. We are telling others that we are not the master of all knowledge. Objectively, we know we should not have all knowledge mastered. No human believes they should know literally everything, as that would be impossible. When our emotional sides get involved, we often FEEL differently. We feel as though not knowing something makes us weak.

When we have a child in front of us who is struggling to learn something new, do we view them as weak? When they give their best attempt then ask for assistance, do we see someone that is a failure? I don't. When I see people giving their all and then asking for help, I see someone who is strong.

Teachers historically viewed themselves as the "sage on the stage," the keeper of all knowledge. Often teachers also fall into the trap of isolation (not independence, but true isolation, where the walls we build around our pedagogical choices are built to protect us from critique, not to foster our self-efficacy). It makes sense then that teachers would be apprehensive about asking for help.

That is where the bravery that Abdelnour talks about comes into play. When we know our limits and speak up, we are being brave. We are being vulnerable and in that space of vulnerability, as we stretch our limits is where we find the most growth.

Putting it All Together

What is one of the best ways to stand alone, know your limits, and the courage to ask for help? Develop a diverse professional learning network (PLN). What do I mean by a diverse PLN? Find others who teach different subjects, grade levels, or roles that vary from yours in some way. Seek educators who have different levels of experience. Include educators from different geographical regions and varied settings (public, private, urban, rural, suburban). Diversity in your PLN ensures you have a variety of viewpoints, experiences, and expertise from which to draw when you need help. It also means you can build up your self-efficacy as you act as a support for others.

A good PLN will allow you to be vulnerable. They will allow you to shine. They will help you to understand yourself and others better. They will be there through this journey, and for that, there is no replacement.

ELIZABETH MERCE IS a kindergarten teacher in Virginia Beach City Public Schools in Virginia Beach, VA where she lives with her husband and daughter. She has been in education for over ten years in roles including classroom teacher, adjunct, mentor, and consultant. She is passionate about all things education with a focus on early childhood and social-emotional learning. You can find her on Twitter, Instagram, Facebook, Voxer, and YouTube by searching @EMercedLearning or EMerced Learning.

Chapter 8

DREAMS ARE BIGGER THAN FEARS

"It's not who you are that holds you back; it's who you think you aren't." — Unknown

---

Everyone has fear. It may not always be present, but it pops up now and then, often when we least expect it. You can feel it creeping in, and it can be hard to shake. I've always had a fear of something, and often, fears of many things. Some of my biggest fears are the fear of failing, of not being able to complete something, and, at times, a fear of public speaking. On occasion, just the thought of a new project or trying to learn something different awakens that "proactive paranoia," and I talk myself out of doing something before even thinking it through, because I told myself that I wouldn't be able to handle it. I convince myself that I don't have the capability to do something before I give myself an opportunity to try. I recognize this more about myself now than I ever did because I see my students doing the same thing. I work to encourage them to give it a go, to cast aside their fear, even though I know too well how hard that can be to do.

I could tell you there are many things I simply cannot do — things that I have never done, but I am well aware of a lack of strength or in skills required, and I know that I would not do well. There are things that I have tried and one way or another, figured out that I'm just not good at them (like jumping from the ski lift), and I am okay with that. I also have a big fear of missing out, not so much in terms of something in the present but rather, in looking toward the future —it's the fear of having missed something in my past. I don't want to question myself later in life, with "I wonder ifs," or "I wonder what could have been." This fear propels me to act, to dive into things, and to take chances. But in doing this, I end up adding a lot to my already full plates (yes multiple), and this kicks my fear of failing into overdrive.

"You gain strength, courage, and confidence by every experience in which you really stop to look fear in the face. You are able to say to yourself, 'I lived through this horror. I can take the next thing that comes along.'" — *Eleanor Roosevelt*

Fear can overwhelm us if we let it. Life is full of challenges, and what might seem small and unimportant to us, to someone else might be the biggest challenge they have ever faced. I have at least one conversation every day that reminds me to keep things in perspective. We need to be mindful of our differences, to welcome other views, and to always do the best that we can with what we know at the time.

We can't be afraid to take chances, to dream big, and to put ourselves out there. That's when great things happen. And the great things that happen might become an unbelievable success story or maybe an epic failure, but either way, it results in an excellent opportunity for learning, growing, and pushing through. It's another story for us to tell that might just be the story someone needs to hear, to help them find their way and to restore hope when they need it the most.

"Every great dream begins with a dreamer. Always remember, you have within you the strength, the patience, and the passion to reach for the stars to change the world." — *Harriet Tubman*

Every great dream begins with
a dreamer. Always remember,
you have within you the strength,
the patience, and the passion
for reaching for the stars to
change the world.
Harriet Tubman

The world amazes me every single day. If you stop to think about all that we have accomplished as a society and question how people came up with a particular idea or dared to take a chance, the world is full of wonder. Look at the progress we've made and continue to make. Imagine how many strong-willed, adventurous, moonshot thinkers took chances to make the world better for others. *Moonshot thinking* is coming up with something like the idea to send astronauts to walk on the moon. As crazy as that seems, not only did someone think about doing that, we figured out how to create the vehicle to propel the astronauts into space and then transport them safely back from the moon. How does that even work? Even more amazing than that is our ability to communicate with astronauts as they move through our universe, landing on the moon 238,000 miles away and being able to see and hear them — amazing capabilities all made possible because of a literal moonshot.

What is a Moonshot?

In May of 1961, President John F. Kennedy spoke of sending astronauts into space by the end of the decade — an idea that people thought impossible, crazy even. This "moonshot" was completed in eight years' time and was the start of more brave expeditions carried out by people working together as a team, dreaming big, accepting failures but not defeat, and persisting until success was achieved. Moonshot takers exhibit bravery, passion, grit, tenacity, and growth mindset — characteristics that we need as educators and that we need to help our students develop. What's the lesson in this moonshot talk?

It's okay to have what you *think* might be a crazy idea, to be filled with doubt, so much in fact that you really don't think that your idea will work. But how will you know until you try it? Of course, you could ask somebody, a colleague, one of your students, a member of your PLN, but what if they tell you that it's not a good idea? Because that's exactly what might happen. They might reinforce or fuel the doubt that you already have in yourself, making you even less likely to take a chance on something. We should value the opinions of those with whom we work and those with whom we lead. It is essential to have those connections. You need to be supported and have relationships where you are comfortable asking somebody for advice or guidance about anything, even those strange or quirky ideas that you might come up with in the middle of the night.

At some point, you must learn to trust your first instinct, quiet that doubt coming from your inner voice, give it a go, cross your fingers, and hope for the best. Take a chance on that moonshot, take a chance on yourself and see what happens. Then, and only then, after you've gone ahead and tried that thing you thought might work, could work, or had little possibility of working, you can reflect on it or reach out to a member of your network and ask for their feedback. They might say that they knew it wasn't a great idea and see why it didn't work. Or maybe it seemed like a great idea, they wonder why it didn't work, and suggest you think about it together. Or it might fall somewhere in between. But you won't get to that point unless you take a chance on that moonshot. As educators, we need to dream big, take those chances and if we're not willing to, then how can we expect that our students will? We are preparing the next generation of innovators, creators, trendsetters, go-getters and moonshot takers. It starts with us.

"Making a moonshot is almost more an exercise in creativity than it is in technology." — *Astro Teller, Captain of Moonshots, Google X*

Remember, we must be the model for our students and not only take those chances but share the risks that we are taking. In pondering the true goals of education, Jean Piaget asked, "Are we forming children who are only capable of learning what is already known? Or should we try to develop creative and innovative minds, capable of discovery from the preschool age on, throughout life?" We absolutely cannot limit what students learn by only conveying the knowledge that we have. It can be scary to think that students might develop skills or acquire knowledge that goes beyond our own, that they might ask a question that we don't know the answer to. (This still bothers me, but I have gotten better with it.) It is an insecurity, but we must be okay with it because we can't limit our students to only what we know. We need for them to grow and to become the designers of our future.

During my eighth grade STEAM course, we discuss different topics and emerging technologies, and one concept we talk about is moonshots." One day in class, I showed a video that Tom Murray had shared with me about the future of learning. When the video ended, two of my students' responses reinforced the WHY behind my interest in talking about moonshots.

I told the class we were going to openly discuss things that we might find to be difficult or frustrating, or something we were curious about. I stressed that it's okay to be afraid to try new things, to not like everything, to find things boring, and to have different opinions. After many years of teaching, I've noticed that some students either feel that they can't or shouldn't say anything negative or shouldn't take a chance if they might fail. Or occasionally the opposite, some students have no problem with expressing their opinion (no filter, as they say) and at times do so in a way that isn't always respectful or mindful of the feelings and comfort of others in the room. Having conversations like this was not something that I often did throughout my career. However, while trying to do things differently and establish better connections between all of us in our classroom, this has become a conversation that I feel I need to have. Why? Because the best learning takes place when students feel supported, comfortable, and welcome in their learning space.

I started by explaining that it is okay to express ourselves about different issues, but it's vital that we (myself included) do so in a respectful way that shows we are listening and responsive to others when they confide in us. An important goal in this is to work on the social-emotional learning (SEL) skills of my students, especially at an early age when there are so many things happening every day in the life of a junior high school student. My motivation is making sure students feel comfortable in class and develop the skills that are so critical for them, such as communication, collaboration, problem-solving, creativity, and empathy.

Trust Must be Built

When I first asked the class if anyone had anything to share, I could see that my students were kind of afraid to speak. It's interesting how sometimes when given the opportunity to share, silence happens, but when it is not the right moment, conversations are flowing. A few minutes passed. Several students kept looking at their peers to see if anyone was going to raise their hand, while at the same time, I was looking around for a volunteer because I was curious to see what they might say. It usually just takes one person to get the conversation going. I was surprised that nobody raised their hand right away when given a chance to speak openly and in what I assured them was a safe space. Maybe they had never been asked this before by their teachers, or by anyone really, to openly vent, for lack of a better word, about anything, even something school-related. I reassured them that it was okay because we were just going to share our ideas. After another minute of silence, I decided to start.

Right when I was going to talk, a few hands went up in the air. One student who was often quiet in class was the first to speak. His question was "Why have we not gone back to the moon? Our technology is way better now —we know so much more, yet we haven't done anything like that for like 30 years!" I was impressed with his willingness to start the conversation, his genuine interest in the topic, and the curiosity he expressed. It was a well-thought-out question/comment that made for a great chat that day. We had fun pondering *what-ifs*, *how comes*, and a lot of *whys*! It also gave me a peek into the interests of a student who, up to that point, had been quiet, kept to himself, and I did not know much about.

"One small step for [a] man, one giant leap for mankind."

This is one of the things I love about my job. Sometimes it only takes the slightest interaction, a quick comment, a thought-provoking question, or just the right catalyst to spark student curiosity and establish a connection with them that will grow and flourish. When we take time to ask questions and are receptive to students' responses, their ideas can lead to exciting and authentic learning that doesn't come out of a textbook and won't be found on a worksheet or in a packet. It's the ideas that are generated by the curiosity that is deep within a student, who is interested in learning even though sometimes students don't demonstrate this. Setting up the right conditions leads to more student-driven questions and times of open wonder that create critical thinkers, problem-solvers, and moonshot takers.

So, this is why we need to take those moonshots, and we need to encourage our students to take moonshots of their own. They need to create and explore their own learning paths, and we must be okay with not being able to answer every question they might come up with. We need to let them ask the questions and create the problems to be solved. We can't possibly know everything —we are as much of learners in the classroom as our students, we just need to keep moving forward.

"*Creativity is not something you get; it's something you reveal.*"

— *Michael Mordechai Cohen (@TheTechRabbi)*

If we want our students to take some risks, to put themselves out there, and experience the discomfort that comes with not knowing all the answers or having fully acquired certain skills, then we must do it too. I was told in ninth grade that I had no artistic ability, so I stayed away from drawing for years. Creativity for me was elusive and often nonexistent. Only recently have I taken some risks, going off the script, and daring to try things that I don't have a lot of experience with, but which I recognize the potential for students. A significant risk was when I started to teach Sketchnoting. I'm a bit uncomfortable while trying to draw icons, especially in front of the class, but it has led to so many positives. I openly share when I am nervous about drawing and have even told the class that I couldn't do it and wouldn't try, only to have *them* encourage *me*. The more we "doodle," the more we learn about each other. Students have said they are not creative, something I have said about myself too. But in this process, we see creativity coming through. And it has been a way for me to learn more about my students, and to foster skills that will benefit them in the future. Making the right decisions about what to teach, how to teach it and everything in between can be tough, but we do the best with what we know at the time.

Decision-Making is Hard

Anyone that knows me whether in "real life" or online knows that I can be a terrible decision-maker. If you ask me to choose one option, I can't decide between even two. If you tell me to pick two, I will give you no less than three. I am and always have been indecisive — partially because I don't like to choose and partially because I'm afraid of making the wrong choice. I've even tried to duck out of a decision by saying, "I'll let you choose," which I thought might work, but in choosing not to respond, that was actually a choice that I made.

For some people, it might seem quite simple to decide between two things. Do you prefer this movie or that one? Ice cream or cake? Which restaurant do you prefer? Sounds simple, but not for me. Maybe my inability to decide even simple things comes from being responsible for daily decisions that not only impact my life, but impact the lives of the students and the colleagues with whom I interact. My decisions typically have the potential to greatly affect many others. This is where my inner struggle comes from. I don't want to make the wrong decision. It can be difficult to understand when to step in and help someone or when just to wait and see what happens with them on their own.

Everyone has fears and doubts and struggles with decision-making. We have a lot of responsibilities, and sometimes maybe the best thing is to start small, take one step, and just keep moving forward.

"Little things make the big things happen." — *John Wooden*

Paul O'Neill
Educator
New Jersey
@pauloneill1972

When it comes to goals, I've always looked to this quote for inspiration. In order to create change on a larger scale, it's important to pay attention to the little things. Paying careful attention to detail transforms behaviors into habits. When these good habits become consistent, lifestyle changes are made. Early in my career, I felt overwhelmed trying to juggle the many responsibilities faced as a novice teacher. Positive change took place once I learned how to commit to a series of mindfulness techniques. Making time for myself, asking for help, reading daily, and frequent reflection became part of the "little things" that made big things happen in my life.

HOW MANY TIMES have you heard students or even colleagues in your school say, "I'm not going to be able to handle all of that" or "it won't make any difference?" How many times have you said it yourself? There is this line of thinking that you either have to "go big or go home" as they say. I believe that to some extent. I think that if you're going to pursue something, then you should give it your all and go for it. But then again, sometimes we may not feel as confident trying something because the thought of putting everything into it at first, knowing that we might fall flat on our face, is too scary and might make us back out of taking on a new challenge.

Everybody makes mistakes and yet there is still a stigma about making them. Does it mean that the person is not good enough or smart enough or capable enough of doing something? No, but for many years we have worried, as a society, about setting standards or goals and it is expected that everyone can meet them, and at the same time. But that isn't the reality. Sometimes we need to marvel at the wonder that happens when even the slightest thing leads to a big change.

SHARE: WHAT IS A MISTAKE YOU MADE THAT LED TO TREMENDOUS PERSONAL OR PROFESSIONAL GROWTH?

#QUOTES4EDU

MY FRIENDSHIP WITH MAUREEN

Maureen is truly a source of positivity, and whenever I hear her share her ideas in our #4OCFPLN, it lifts me up and inspires me to do more. She is an advocate for student choice, for taking risks and for doing whatever it takes to create an authentic, meaningful learning experience for students and teachers. I know that her WHY is to provide exactly what each student needs, and to do so, she invests herself in providing the right learning opportunities for educators, so they can, in turn, do what's best for each of their learners.

Chapter 9

"WHAT IS BEST FOR THIS LEARNER?"

MAUREEN HAYES

"What is best for this learner?" — George Couros

As educators, our number one priority is to ensure our students' academic success. Academic success is often interpreted differently across the realm of education and educators, but the learner must be at the forefront of all decisions.

Keeping in mind developmental readiness and appropriateness, what are our expectations for growth at each grade level?

What demonstrates sufficient academic growth?

This Learner's Data Story

As we look to make instructional decisions to best support each student, we need to gather a deep understanding of each student's data story. No one data point should be used solely for instructional decisions, aside from strand data used to form small groups for guided practice or strategy groups.

Each student has a data story, which includes a variety of assessment data collected through formative and summative assessments, as well as teacher observations and anecdotal notes, and let's not forget self-assessment and SEL (Social Emotional Learning) needs. All this information needs to be used when making instructional decisions, meeting the students where they are and working on getting them where they need to be.

This Learner's Journey

It is vital that students play an integral part in their academic journey. They need to be responsible for their own learning and monitoring their own progress, but this only happens if we provide students the opportunity to do so. We need to provide students with the power and guidance for setting their own goals and monitoring their progress towards these goals.

Students need to keep track of the goals they set and frequently meet with their teachers to reflect and discuss progress. The teacher can offer support and additional resources, and even guide students towards specific goals as they observe a need.

Students can play a vital role in the assessment process if we empower them through self-assessment and determining criteria for assessment. Make students aware of lesson objectives and have them reflect on their progress. As educators, we need to make sure our goals are transparent for students, sharing these at the start and conclusion of lessons.

This Learner's Academic Readiness

As a former primary teacher, I know the importance of academic readiness. However, I also firmly believe in the importance of developmental appropriateness, and in an era of "push-down curriculum," more and more is being expected from our students, beginning in kindergarten with our five- and six-year-olds.

Here is an analogy I often share with preschool and kindergarten parents:

When a child is learning to walk, the process can begin as early as nine months of age or as late as 14 months of age. We've all watched a child in their journey towards mobility, and one thing I think we can agree on is that the process cannot be rushed. If you take a child who is not yet ready for their first steps and stand them up, they will fall. No matter how many times you repeat this process, the child will tumble as their bodies are not yet ready to support this new progression. Conversely, I know that you can't get in the way of a child who is ready and determined to take those first steps. Look out, because here they come!

My daughter walked at nine months of age, and her cousin didn't walk until fourteen months. They are now both adults, and no one has ever looked at them as said, "She is a good walker! She must have been an early walker! Oh, look at him. I bet he didn't walk until after he turned one."

The answer is a resounding no. They each walked when each was developmentally ready to do so, and it wasn't the result of pushing the process along or helping my daughter to walk early. Both children had bouncy seats and walking toys to support them along their journey, but "extra practice" was not the difference, and they did not demonstrate any developmental delays.

We can also apply this analogy to reading. We must provide rich experiences on the road to reading through exposure to books and words and print, but the pieces will come together on their own time. For some children, this is in kindergarten, but for most, it occurs in first grade. For a few students, it may not happen until second grade. The important thing is for us as educators to be there to support our students, picking them up when they fall.

In a society of Common Core Standards as well as state and district mandates, many educators are pushing down curriculum and interpreting the rigor of standards without considering what is developmentally appropriate. In school districts across the country, kindergarten students are being assessed on sight words in January with the additional expectation of reading at a first-grade level. These children are being set up for failure.

There does come a time when we can begin to ask questions concerning our students:

- When do we go beyond meeting them where they are and looking at other possibilities affecting student growth?
- When do we look at the possibility of developmental delays or even a learning difference?

This is where the student's data story comes into play. Look at the progress made and begin to determine if the growth is steady and significant, or if it is time to look at other possibilities that may be interfering with learning.

This Learner's Right to Play and Explore

Now that brings me to the importance of play and other experiences for our earliest learners. I firmly believe that kindergarten and part of the primary grades need to continue to be a place of readiness. Let's not lose sight of the journey of childhood and the time our children need.

It's a time to develop essential social-emotional and executive function skills.

…a time to play, wonder, explore and question.

…a time to make friends and learn to understand differences.

…a time to follow directions, cut, color, paint, and glue.

…a time to learn about numbers and patterns in the world through meaningful, real-life experiences.

…a time to draw and learn how to properly hold a pencil as they practice forming letters and numbers.

It's a time to rhyme, learn letters and their corresponding sounds, and concepts about print.

All of this is in preparation for learning to read, write, and develop number sense in first grade and beyond. Accelerating this process will not produce "better students," but can impact their sense of wonder and lead to frustration for those who are not developmentally ready.

We need to stop pushing down curriculum, but work to make experiences developmentally appropriate and rich with real-world applications.

Let them play, for it is through this that a true learner will emerge — one who never stops wondering, questioning, and persevering.

This Learner's Voice and Choice

Last spring, I participated in a book study with #2menandabook on Rebecca Coda and Rick Jetter's book, *Let Them Speak*. I am a strong advocate for student voice and choice in the classroom, and the book sparked me to carry this conversation with students beyond the walls of the classroom to the curriculum level.

Inspired by the book and the conversations in the book study, I set out to interview the students in my district about my curriculum...the elementary language arts curriculum.

I kept the interviews short and sweet, just five questions:

1. What is your favorite subject in school?
2. What do you like best about reading in school?
3. What do you like best about writing in school?
4. If you were in charge of reading and writing in your classroom, what would you do differently from your teacher?
5. Aside from lunch and recess, what do you wish you had more time for during the school day?

Next, I spent a few weeks visiting every first- through sixth-grade classroom in my district, interviewing two random students (a boy and a girl) in each classroom. I opted not to interview kindergarten students at this time due to the developmental appropriateness of the questions. In all 160 students were interviewed.

So, what did I learn from this process? What were my takeaways?

First and foremost was the affirmation of the importance of student voice and choice in their learning.

Of the 160 students interviewed, 46.6% (75) shared that math is their favorite subject. Reading was the second highest subject selected at 17.4%, followed by writing at 9.9%. This question is one I'm going to need to take a closer look at and find why students enjoy math so much. Since this process had a focus on our ELA curriculum, I pushed forward.

Next, it was time to sort and analyze the rest of the data. The data was full of answers that connected to student voice and choice. Fifty-nine out of the 160 students interviewed (37%) stated in some form that their favorite part of reading is independent reading. This is the time each day when students self-select books from their classroom or school library and students are provided with quiet reading time.

Several students also talked about how the quiet classroom during independent reading time makes it their favorite time of the day.

That got me thinking about some classrooms that can be overly stimulating for our students through the decorations or noise. This emphasizes the need to include student voice and choice in the classroom environment with setting up and decorating the classroom.

More revealing was the answer to students' favorite part about writing. Ninety students (56%) stated that they liked writing stories when they get to make up their own stories or guide their own ideas for writing. Students like having choice in their writing.

Nowhere in student responses did anyone talk about tests, worksheets, or packets, and very few answers spoke to teacher-led learning. Most students prefer to guide their own learning when the teacher gives them voice with guidance and support.

This student interview process provided me with a lot of data to sort through, analyze, share with staff, and use to reflect on my role as a curriculum supervisor. Some of the more poignant moments came in the heartfelt answers from students. When asked what she wished there was more time for in school each day, one sixth grade girl responded, "Fun. School used to be fun." Wow! Several other students commented on their wish for more choice time, free time, centers, technology, and even independent reading.

This is the second year I have interviewed students about school, and I thoroughly enjoy the process. Not only do I enjoy the conversations with kids, but they speak the truth...I can learn a lot from listening to them. Students continually affirm my belief in the importance of voice and choice in guiding their own learning.

This Learner's Right to Academic Success

We must always keep what is best for the learner at the forefront of decision-making in schools. It is our number one responsibility and commitment as educators to provide an environment where each student feels safe and loved, and above all, in the care of adults who believe in them and their success.

Each student must be looked at individually. The days of teaching to the average are long past. There is no average when it comes to our students. Each child has an individual story and their own path towards learning. It is our responsibility to meet each child where they are and set goals for moving forward. It is our responsibility always to do "what is best for the learner."

This Learner's Right to a Significant Relationship with Teachers

"Fair is not always equal" is an essential phrase for education. I have met educators throughout my journey who make two vital mistakes when it comes to meeting the needs of their students.

The first mistake is found in the phrase, "that's how I've always done it." When we know better, we do better, and as we continually discover ways to best meet the needs of the diverse students that we have in our classrooms, we need to change the way we do things. As we learn more about the importance of social-emotional learning, toxic stress, trauma and Adverse Childhood Experiences (ACEs) in our students, we know that we need to meet each learner where they are and support SEL needs before we can even begin to expect significant academic growth.

We know that some students will need additional scaffolding on their path to academic success, and whether this is through modifications, test retakes, additional small group, or independent instruction, we need to provide our students with the best path to learning for THEM, and this will look different for each student. Just because something is taught does not mean it is learned by all, and teachers need to reflect on student data and progress to determine each student's needs. Differentiation is not an option, but an expectation.

Mistake #2 comes in the rigidity of classroom rules and policies, and some teachers' unwillingness to makes changes in the best interest of the student. This is where it becomes imperative that as educators, we check our egos at the door.

Just because it is "not the way we've always done things" does not mean we should arbitrarily deny a parent request for something that is in the best interest of the child. We need to listen to parent concerns and requests. We may not always honor them, but an open mind is necessary for determining what is best for each student.

We must ensure that our students have the necessary tools needed for success, both academically and social-emotionally. Our students are our future, and our schools need to be a safe place for them to question, wonder, and even struggle as they grow towards adulthood. Above all, we need to ensure that every decision we make is what is best for this learner.

Maureen is an Elementary Humanities Supervisor for Lawrence Township Public Schools in Lawrenceville, NJ. Over her 25 years in education, she has been both a first- and second-grade teacher as well as a reading specialist before becoming a curriculum supervisor.

Maureen publishes the blog Kids First: Passionate Leadership and is a member of the International Reading Association and the #4OCFpln. She is passionate about early literacy and supporting each child's academic as well as social-emotional needs while putting relationships first.

PART II

"Before you are a leader, success is all about growing yourself. When you become a leader, success is all about growing others."

– Jack Welch, former GE chairman and CEO

MY FRIENDSHIP WITH DON

Don is a member of the #4OCFPLN, like many of the guest authors, and there are so many lessons that I have learned from him by being connected. So much of what he shares in his chapter resonates with me as well. When he chose his quotes and shared his story, I could not wait to share it with others.

Chapter 10

TEACHING MORE THAN CONTENT

DON STURM

"Strong teachers don't teach content; Google has content. Strong teaching connects learning in ways that inspire kids to learn more and strive for greatness." — Eric Jensen

---

"Too often we give children answers to remember rather than problems to solve." — Roger Lewin

---

It will probably come as no surprise to practicing educators that a significant debate exists in schools today about the role teachers play in conveying facts and content to students. As with any topic worthy of discussion, the issue is complex, and teachers' feelings fall along a continuum. On one end of this continuum are the teachers who look to the nostalgia of the past and wish to deliver to students the same type of education that they received. These educators view the role of the teacher as the "content expert." Those at the other end of the spectrum hold beliefs that schools need to be places where students are individually challenged and ultimately responsible for their own education. These teachers feel it is vital to help guide or facilitate student learning, not to be the only person sharing content or facts.

As an educator for 28 years, I have moved along this continuum out of necessity. At the start of my career, content knowledge was not as readily available; I needed to be the content expert. The world that our students must navigate has changed. Knowledge and content are more widely available, and as a result, I have felt the need to keep up with those changes. My almost 30 years in education has allowed me to see the impact of time and advancement on a profession for which I am passionate.

For a minute let's imagine the obituary for a person who lived from 1890 to 1970. When they were born, the world was newly electrified, and horse and buggy were the dominant means of transport. When this person turned 13-years-old, humans took flight for the first time as the Wright Brothers flew their Wright Flyer at Kitty Hawk, North Carolina. In this person's 30s, the car became an integral part of the culture of the United States. In the person's 37th year of life, Charles Lindbergh became the first person to fly solo across the Atlantic Ocean. Once the person reached the ripe old age of 67, the Soviets launched Sputnik, the first human-made satellite to orbit the earth, and in their 79th year, they saw humans land on the moon.

It is very easy to detail the type of changes that occurred during this period, but it becomes mind-boggling to think about the actual impact of these changes. Changes were fast and furious, and people struggled to keep up with these changes that they were witnessing. And it is not surprising that there were individuals who did not like this fast-paced change, but it happened, nonetheless.

So how does this little history lesson relate to education? The changes that I have seen in my 28-year career are similar to the radical changes that the person above lived through during their 80 years. The world is a much different place than when I stepped foot in my first classroom.

Graduating from high school in 1987 and enrolling in college as a history major meant a lot of research and writing. Countless hours were spent at Milner Library at Illinois State University finding information that I needed to back up and support whatever topic I was researching. This information was not easily obtained. The *Reader's Guide to Periodical Literature* was my friend or my nemesis, depending on the subject. I would find an article that I thought would be helpful, fill out a slip of paper to request this article, and wait for the librarian to head to the depths of the library to find it. Many times, the information I asked for was not helpful, and I would start my search again. This was my life for the four years of my undergraduate coursework. Information was difficult and time-consuming to obtain.

As I started my teaching career in 1991, the main sources of information for teachers and students were textbooks, magazines, newspapers, and books. Knowledge was not readily available, and most of what students used as sources of information were provided by the teacher. I assigned research projects for which students were expected to consult outside sources obtained from the local library, but these sources were few and far between. The requirements for sources related only to the types and number of source materials that needed to be consulted. Honestly, the textbook was the major source of information for students. As additional content was required, the lecture became the dominant mode of instruction in my classroom. I like to think that I am a good storyteller, but ultimately, class consisted of students taking notes on the necessary information. Students were expected to present, apply, and discuss, but the information was usually gleaned from packets that I had put together. The important point here: I was the provider of most of the information that students consumed. I was the *sage on the stage.*

The choice of how to present material at the start of my career was limited. Of course, there were copy machines (I came just a little late for the mimeograph), chalkboards, pull-down wall maps, filmstrips, and a TV/VCR combo on a cart that had to be checked out well in advance. I had no overhead projector until my third year of teaching. I occasionally made use of the opaque projector during my first three years. For those of you who are not familiar with said machine, it was a giant monstrosity with mirrors and a bulb with brightness the likes of the sun that produced an image on a pull-down screen. Most days of class consisted of me being in the front of the room sharing my knowledge of whatever topic we were covering. Sure, we discussed, role-played, and argued topics, but again, it was mostly on my terms, and with content I had chosen.

It is essential to keep in mind that this was the life of most teachers. We did not think about it much because it was just how it was done. Schools in 1991 were very much like the schools of many of the previous decades. Teaching strategies and philosophies might have changed over that time, but the way content was presented had not changed much. I started to notice the possibility of change toward the end of my first year. I received a 2400 baud modem for Christmas 1991, and with it came significant changes. This modem (think a REALLY slow dial-up connection) changed the way that I looked at the world and the content that I was teaching. I could log into America Online and get information from news sources that could then be shared with the students. No longer did I have to trek to the library to get more information than the textbook could provide; information was literally at my fingertips. Most teachers and students did not have access yet, and there were no school connections at this point, but the access to knowledge was being turned upside down. I was still the content expert choosing information that I would share with my students, but there was so much more from which to choose. Little did I know that I was in the first group of teachers who were using the Internet for their classes.

Access to computers also changed radically after the mid-1990s. The Internet became more a staple of life and computers became part of the usual toolbox for teachers. The district where I currently work added a computer lab where we could schedule classes. At first, that time in the computer lab was not hard to get, but as time marched on, more and more teachers came to use the lab as a way to extend what they had been teaching. Not everyone saw the benefit of this new age of learning. Many teachers still reserved the computer lab for the sole purpose of typing papers. I can remember being frustrated wanting to use the online version of the CIA Factbook to teach World Geography but having to think so far ahead to gain computer lab time. In 1998, I asked the district to buy a classroom set of Microsoft's Encarta Virtual Globe as a supplement for my geography curriculum. The kids and I were amazed at the capabilities of this CD-ROM program. We could all be taken on a flyover of a variety of countries and regions and view pictures and statistics that seem so readily available today. My past lectures on areas of the world could not compete with students visually engaging with the content. It was an exciting time to be a teacher.

The ability to present information in an exciting fashion changed at this time as well. In 1994, my department head asked me what I would like added to my classroom wish list. My response: a laserdisc player (think giant CD) with a barcode scanner that allowed me to access tens of thousands of photos. It might be hard to imagine, but this revolutionized my classroom. No longer did I have to rely on taking color photos from National Geographic and make them into black and white overheads to show students. We could access pictures from all over the world by scanning a barcode. Teacher computers were added a few years later and again, while PowerPoints are probably overused today, at the time they made the presentation of material so much more interesting for the student. PowerPoint also became the norm for student presentations. No longer was the poster, which could not be seen by anyone beyond the front row, the go-to during a presentation. With so many students and teachers needing more than a chalkboard to present, the addition of the LCD projector became commonplace in classrooms.

While the progression that started in the mid-1990s was revolutionary, it was still primarily focused on what the teacher could do differently. We have now moved into the period where the available technology has changed the way that students interact with information. Information is so readily available that the teacher no longer needs to be the *sage on the stage*. This shift does not mean that teacher content expertise no longer matters, only that the primary role of the teacher has changed from that of sharing and delivering content to designing valuable learning experiences. The roles and responsibilities of teachers have changed dramatically since I started teaching. Teachers, whether new or seasoned, need to accept that times have changed, and as a result, our methods need to change. We are doing our current students a disservice if we continue to teach the way that we were taught. The students of today will enter a workforce that is much different than the one I entered when I was fresh out of college. Students must be challenged to tackle the real-world problems that are present in today's world. Content and information are just as relevant now as they have been, but teachers are no longer the holders and providers of knowledge as they were in the past.

The first steps in this retooling of the educational system should be focused on the skills students need, rather than what content teachers are expected to present. Some will stop me right there and comment that students need facts and content more than ever. I would argue that they do not necessarily need the content as much as they need the ability to sort through and judge all of the content that is available to them online. If teachers continue to just broadcast content, students will not learn how to navigate the plethora of information that they are flooded with daily. If we are completely honest with ourselves, students do not remember the specific content that is being taught as much, as they are going through the motions of school. We should strive to make school a place where students want to be, not just a place that they go because that is what has always been done. Relevancy is something that students crave, not content. With that being said, content should be the vehicle by which we teach the skills that are part of the standards being taught. I do not agree with the naysayers who claim that this new educational paradigm shift discounts content at the expense of skills. The skills focus gives the material more meaning to students.

So how does this change happen in your school and classroom?

This question is difficult to answer because of all the grade levels and subject matters involved. Schools, teachers, students, and community members need to start conversations about what education means in today's world. The one aspect that everyone can hopefully agree on is that schools cannot be what they were in the past. We must stop arguing about what 21st-Century skills look like and start teaching those skills, since we are eighteen plus years into the new century! It does not matter whether you like or dislike our society and culture; it is the one that our students are living in, and we do them an injustice if we do not teach them the skills that will be needed when they walk out of the school on graduation day.

The change happens when you realize that school must be different. When that realization hits, talk with your colleagues and start planning for how this change impacts you and your curriculum. Be an advocate for change that will be beneficial for students, not what is best and easiest to teach. There are numerous books available for you to get ideas of what change might look like in your classroom. If you hit roadblocks with your colleagues, become active on social media to find those teachers and administrators who will help you make the changes. For me, Twitter and Voxer have connected me with like-minded individuals who push my pedagogical thinking. There is so much help and wisdom from practicing teachers if you are willing to spend the time to make connections. The key is that as educators who care about the students we are teaching, we need to take the initiative to change the system to one that is better suited for the world that our students inhabit.

The quotes that started this chapter share the reality of the world in which we live. Times change and schools need to change as well. Education is too important to continue with practices that while they worked in the past are not what students need for today.

Educators have a responsibility to make sure that schools are places that inspire students to solve real-world problems. While there might be many ways to reach this goal, one thing is for sure: students must play a bigger role in their own education. This more significant role will help students learn their passions, which will help to guide their future endeavors. All those involved in education, from the teachers to the community, need to take on the responsibility of changing the system so that students are given a more relevant educational experience.

DON STURM IS *a Technology Integration Specialist for Morton CUSD #709 in Morton, IL. Prior to this position, he was a social studies teacher for 23 years. His passion has always been the role that technology plays in schools as well as the change that comes with the introduction of technology. He can be found on Twitter at @sturmdon and he blogs at schoolscanbebetter.com.*

Chapter 11

KNOWING MORE THAN US

"Learning is finding out what you already know. Doing is demonstrating that you know it. Teaching is reminding others that they know it just as well as you. You are all learners, doers, teachers." — Richard Bach, American Writer

We have an essential job to do every single day, and it's not just teaching the content. With every passing year, there are new initiatives, ideas, strategies, and demands on our time, so keeping balance and staying relevant in our work can be a challenge. It's easy to lose our passion when we lose focus on our purpose. We can work around this by becoming more connected and developing our own personal and professional learning networks. Even with so much access literally in the palm of our hands, it still takes the ever-elusive time to make those connections, to ask questions, and to put into action any of the ideas that we receive. So, what can we do? How can we stay relevant and provide what we need to do more for our students, so they can succeed in the future with whatever it is that they ultimately decide to do?

We do more than teach. We learn with students. We learn from them. We learn about them. And we become okay with the discomfort we might feel when we don't have an answer, or times that students might pick up on something faster than we do. That's the way it's supposed to be. Limiting students to our own knowledge will not benefit them in the future. It will deplete curiosity and critical thinking and focus only on products of learning rather than the process. When we don't intentionally push ourselves to acquire more knowledge and invest ourselves in our work, keeping sight of our purpose and our passion for what we do, we can become disengaged. If we disengage, then we lose our way. When we lose our way, our work and passion for teaching diminish.

As leaders, we must have the courage to take those first steps, to stand after we fall, and to create a path that leads students to the success they are destined for. It does not always come by covering content and following curriculum. We use the world as our classroom and inspire students to seek knowledge that matters to them. We stop teaching a "class" and teach students, in ways that enable us to reach and engage different learners that we may miss in the traditional classroom design. We must put students first and be learner-centered and driven. But what does that look like and where do we begin?

"Times and conditions change so rapidly that we must keep our aim constantly focused on the future." — *Walt Disney*

Jon Craig
Instructional Coach
Harry S. Truman High School
Bristol Township School District
@coachjoncraig

Technology in the classroom can do many things. It can provide the voice for a student who may be physically unable or gripped with anxiety. It can translate for our non-English speaking populations. It can knock down the walls of any classroom and connect our students with students and experts all over the world. There are not many things that technology can't do, but replacing a great teacher is one of those things it can't.

Google and YouTube have an overabundance of content, but on their own, they cannot perform the multiple tasks a great teacher performs on any given day. Building relationships, providing specific, actionable feedback, adjusting lessons in real time, and getting students precisely what they need are just a few tasks that make great teachers irreplaceable. When strong teachers include these tools in their practice, the combination of practice and technology leads to learning experiences that inspire, empower, and motivate students to strive for greatness. We owe it to our students to overcome our apprehensions, fears, and hesitations towards technology, as we confidently use technology to support us, not replace us.

———

SOMETIMES I WONDER how much time educators spend writing lesson plans, developing curriculum or designing activities, projects, and creating assessments for their classrooms. I don't know that it's even possible to guess anywhere close to the amount of time that is spent on all these activities, as well as all of the thinking involved in our role as educators. For many years, I felt like I was in a race against the clock, thinking that I had to get through the textbook. I had to cover the content, write lengthy lesson plans, regularly give tests, projects, and homework. If students would interject with a side story or fall off task briefly to talk to a friend or to tell me a story about something, I was quick to put an end to it. It's not that it bothered me, and it's not that there was anything wrong with it — it's just the way I had been taught. Teachers did not share stories with students. Lessons lasted from bell to bell; while the teaching methods used by each teacher may have differed, these aspects of teaching did not. As I worked toward my education degree in college, our class time was spent focusing on the "how" to cover the content and we were reminded to use every minute and teach to the bell. What didn't get completed in class went home to be done for the next day, and the cycle repeated itself. Every single day. Moving by the bell.

Going with what I knew best (which was what I had experienced as a student), this is what I did in my classroom for many years. I tried to create enough activities to keep students busy, which is different than "actively learning." I know it doesn't sound great now, but to get through some days, I felt like I had to keep them busy and that I had to be "on stage" for the entire period. A lot of that time was spent with me talking, giving instructions, or writing examples on the board and not noticing that students were talking, drawing, reading, or maybe even sleeping while I taught. They weren't actively involved. It was all me. Only when I would find pictures drawn in their notebooks did I start to realize they were tuning me out (some did not have the notes I gave). I was talking *at* them, and I didn't notice because I stayed in the front, facing the board, writing, and not interacting with them or moving around the classroom as I should have been.

I had opportunities to learn about them when they completed projects, and I could get an idea of their likes and dislikes, learn about their families or favorite activities. But it's not that I had a genuine understanding of *who* they were — knowing "what" they did in their free time or which school activities they were involved in didn't help me to truly know them or connect with them. Without understanding their interests or their passions, knowing only simple facts did not lead to a meaningful connection. It also didn't let my students know that I cared more about them and their well-being than about the content itself. I just didn't "plan" for conversations between us in the classroom because I needed every minute of every period to cover the curriculum from the book (or so I thought).

It's not like I'm talking about ten years ago —it was closer to three or four when I began to shift. I remember writing a schedule on the board, so students knew what to expect during class, and I thought that was good enough. Students often asked me about my weekend or how my break was, and I would cut the conversation short by saying "it was good, how was yours?" and shift the conversation because I *had* to start teaching the content, the time was ticking away. But today, at least over the past few years, thankfully through connections I have made, I have learned that there is so much more to teaching than simply what is covered in the book or the course. Teaching involves many things, way beyond what teachers did in the past. I think the biggest part of it is knowing that it's okay to learn about the students and it's okay to connect what we are teaching to their lives and their experiences. The encouragement of a supportive mentor helped me to understand the importance of getting to know the kids.

Don't talk to me...can't we just talk?

Now there are days where I get caught up in some conversations with my students. I genuinely enjoy talking with them, learning about their experiences in other classes, and learning about them in general. By understanding more about who they are, I can develop better-suited teaching strategies that will lead to more meaningful learning. The STEAM course that I teach is a favorite of mine because I loved technology as a child, and I continue to be fascinated by all that it makes possible. And while I appreciate the wondrous capabilities of it, I'm also very much aware that technology is not the answer to everything. It has to be purposeful, and there are just some times where technology is the catalyst that gets students excited for learning or engages them a little bit more in the content and the class. What I have found to be even greater than this are the simple conversations that can and should happen regularly in our classrooms.

I Had to Ask

During the first couple weeks of school, students were completely drained because of excessive heat outside and the non-functioning cooling system inside the building. It reminded me of my own high school years when we did not have air conditioning at all, and just sitting still wore us out. One Friday afternoon, I had my plans set for my STEAM class. It was one of my favorite lessons, where I show old technology and act out what it was like to carry some of these things around, or the long process it sometimes took to acquire information. (think Walkman radios and rotary phones). I was waiting at the door with my Walkman, and as students entered, I could see they were entirely drained. As excited as I was for this lesson and to show these old 80s devices, I recognized that a new plan was needed. I decided just to talk with them. I was curious about how their new school year was going and started by acknowledging that I knew it was hot and that everyone was tired, but that we had to keep going. I told them I would save the planned lesson, and instead we would just talk. This took them by surprise. One of my main goals is to let students know that I support them. I want them to feel comfortable in our classroom, free to share their ideas, experiences, and yes, even their frustrations at times.

"Different people have different opinions, and it's okay to respect all of them." — *Juan Pablo Galavis*

We must teach students how to interact with others and the importance of being respectful even when we don't agree with someone or have a difference in opinion. We must emphasize accepting one another, being able to have a conversation, even the difficult ones, and feeling safe to express what's on your mind, by doing so in a way that each person feels valued and respected. So, I said to the class, "Let's talk about complaints. I want to know what is on your mind, and then we will see where it goes from there." They thought I was joking, I assured them that I was not, and then each of the nine students took a minute or two to talk about some of their frustrations during the first two weeks of school. Many said classes were boring (most common complaint); that each class was the same; all they did was sit, listen, and take notes, class after class, every single day. Their words hit me hard because that is exactly how I had been teaching and had been taught in many classes, until I made changes a few years ago.

"Life can be boring unless you put some effort into it."

— *John C. Maxwell*

I must have had a certain look on my face because a few students quickly said, "not your class Mrs. Poth," to which I responded that it was okay if they included my class because I would prefer that they tell me that something was not working, or didn't go as well as maybe it could have. I tried to give an example by saying instead of telling a teacher, "Your class is so boring," first think about why it seems that way. Rather than making a statement like that, why not suggest a different activity or a game? Just like students need feedback to grow in our classes, we are learners and need to grow in our teaching practices. I said it's okay to let others know that you might not be having the best experience ever, but there is a right way and a wrong way to go about doing that. I suggested that sometimes they need to advocate for themselves. For example, maybe they could recommend playing a game for practice or instead of writing lengthy notes, try something like sketchnoting. I explained that while we won't always have the same excitement for learning or feel the same about class activities, it is good to remember that teachers are teaching content that they are passionate about. My hope was that students would view school and learning a bit differently, and perhaps appreciate that teachers want to use their knowledge to help others. I told them we all have something to teach and a lot of things to learn. By sharing our ideas like we did that day, the students learned more about each other, and I definitely learned a lot more about them. And there was a different vibe to the room — hard to put into words, but easy to see and feel.

The "Lesson" Can Wait

One thing I've learned is that sometimes it's good to hold off on the content for another two or three minutes (or longer) and do something out of the ordinary, maybe like taking a class field trip to the water fountain. Why? Because we all felt the same, the classroom was so hot, and three students had already gone to the water fountain, two more asked to go, and one wanted to go to the restroom, which I interpreted would include a stop by the water fountain during the hallway adventure anyway. So yes, I took my class on a very short field trip into the cool hallway to let everyone get a drink from the fountain. I even encouraged them to get one more drink just in case, before we returned to our classroom. Taking a break like this, a brain break, is good for social-emotional learning. My friend Laura Steinbrink (@SteinbrinkLaura) has taught me some brain break strategies, and this is one of them, but I did not realize it at the time. It just seemed like a good idea. It was and it made a difference in energy and attitudes.

When we got back to the room, I still had enough time to talk about old technology, show a short "Kids React to Walkmans" video and pass around old cell phones. What fun seeing the looks on their faces when I turned the lights on and had an old "cell phone in a shoulder bag." If only I had a camera to record their reactions, it would have made for a great new video of "Kids react to old cell phones!" This lesson was not heavy on content, and most of it was not layered within some embedded curriculum, but it made for a great day of learning. I learned about the students, their interests, and they learned that it's okay to ask questions, to question methods and ideas, to ask WHY. It's more about *how* we question things because the goal is to communicate and collaborate.

Years ago, I never would have done this, but sometimes you have to push that content out of the way and swap it for time to learn about the students. I think that might just be one of my favorite days ever. I told them not to count on random field trips every day, but I said it seemed like just what they needed at that time. It was a random activity that worked because we came back together feeling refreshed and ready to push through.

"I think the only way for you to grow and evolve is to keep listening, keep moving forward, keep jumping in and trying to experience."

— *Dianne Reeves*

Just Go with It

Doing things off the script does not come easy. For many years I've worried about having a detailed daily plan, covering the objectives listed on the board, following the book's curriculum, or using what seemed to be proper pacing because that's the way I've always done it or the way I learned. Finally, I've made changes and think I'm going in the right direction. I've been throwing around different ideas in my mind under two mantras: "Lean in and Listen" and "Just Go with It." Not that I think we should make it a regular practice to go into our classrooms without a plan, but I seriously think there are great benefits to either not having a solid plan or just abandoning the plan at some point. Why? Because when you have a plan that doesn't go exactly as you hope, or something pops up in the middle of it (like a fire drill, phone call, power outage, students stopping in to say hi, or someone breaks your new Don Quixote bobblehead), that hiccup in the plan can quickly lead to stress. So, my idea is once in a while instead of having a plan, lean in and listen to students' ideas and focus on their needs. Just kind of "go with it," and learning might happen in better ways that exceed what the most well-thought-out plan could have.

One day as I was preparing to teach about virtual reality (one of my favorite things to teach) in my eighth-grade STEAM course, as students came in, there was absolute silence. I noticed that half of them were looking at their phones, maybe texting or choosing a song, looking at pictures, playing a game, or all of the above. There were no interactions, no conversations, just phone-focused, a common sight in schools. Not a single student was taking a selfie or on Snapchat, everyday occurrences in other classes with the older students. The point of this is that it always surprises me how many students have access to technology at such a young age. One of my favorite things about teaching this class is that it reminds me of when I was the same age, although it was 1984 (unbelievable that 35 years have gone by). Sometimes seeing their activities and making comparisons to when I was their age helps me to make connections with them. It leads to the creation of a more innovative, authentic classroom experience for us all.

I absolutely love that feeling of going back in time to share what the technology was like and how we communicated in high school. My students and I have fun trying to predict the future by comparing it to the changes that I have seen in my lifetime. I am curious about the trends and technologies that will develop over the next 20 to 30 years, although I hope it does not go as fast as the past 35 years have gone. The students ask so many questions, and the conversations definitely stray from *my* original plan, but the learning that results (about ourselves and the world) goes far beyond what I could have planned for or hoped. By asking about their access to technology, what devices their families have, what they have seen, and then finding ways to connect it to our collective experiences, technology becomes something that we can share and talk about together. It becomes a class full of wonder.

"Technology is just a tool. In terms of getting the kids working together and motivating them, the teacher is most important."

— *Bill Gates*

WHEN I ASK students to name one tool that can be used to communicate, to take a photo, and to look up information, the answer is invariably a cell phone. But if I were to go back and ask my eighth-grade self that same question, I would have to name three different objects:

1. I did not have my own **phone** as a child,
2. I did not own a **camera** until I was a junior in high school (I lost it on a field trip by the way), and
3. **Computers** were still very basic and there was no internet. Research was done at the library using books.

You see, we needed landline phones, actual cameras with rolls of film waiting to be developed, and time-consuming research was done in a local library. For today's students, that seems so antiquated. Any information they need is accessible right in the palm of their hand. But for those of us 70s and 80s kids, we needed multiple devices or traveled to libraries, and it took longer to obtain information and communicate.

To teach about these tools, I could have students use their phones or iPads to find videos or pictures of old computers, rotary phones, or Walkman radios. Students could research how these technologies developed, their costs, and how people used them. They can instantly find all kinds of information, never-ending resources with images, videos, websites, old commercials, and much more. But learning needs to go beyond the "look it up, define it and move on," or just "Google it." This does not give students an authentic or meaningful experience. But creating a "blast from the past" activity, where I show an old piece of technology and give students time to explore it and laugh with them about the advancements, has made a difference. They pondered what it would be like to actually talk using a rotary phone, having to stand or sit in a limited space because of the short cord, repeatedly dialing if there was a busy signal during the call. The funniest time was when I greeted students passing by my room while holding the phone and telling them they had a phone call. Most of them had no idea what it was, and some stopped to get a look and pretend to make a call. Many were fascinated by the spin and clicking sound of the rotary and wanted to plug it into the wall to see if they could call their cell phone. They were curious, engaged, and thankful that they don't have to use rotary phones, and that phones today do way more than just dial a number. Fun, connected, meaningful, and purposeful learning — not from a video, nor a book, but a more open, hands-on, active, and collaborative learning experience for students. Without a script.

By not having to adhere to a textbook or a stringent curriculum, I started the year by just jumping in, having some fun, and seeing where the learning took them and me. I was eager for the start of each class each day, and the questions they would come up with along the way. Unscripted, off the course of the plan, is sometimes the most powerful form of learning. I feel like no matter what I intend to teach them during class, I walk away having been taught so much more. I facilitate their learning, and I'm good with that.

"I've always tried to go a step past wherever people expected me to end up." — Beverly Sillis

---

Sometimes you do have to take some chances, maybe because you have a feeling or an instinct that there's a better way to do it, that might break from the norm. But we must push the limit when it's the best for our students; we take that extra step.

I asked a friend of mine, Dr. Toutoule Ntoya, to tell me about some of his teaching experiences and I've done my best to retell his story, as he told it to me.

Dr. Toutoule Ntoya
Instructional Coach
Pasadena, CA
@toutoulentoya
www.toutoulentoya.com

One year I had a bunch of honors classes, and one thing I figured out about my honors kids was that even though they were eager and more willing to do the work, they still had a lot of gaps in terms of their willingness to be self-motivated.

I got into a lot of trouble with this, but I just finished my credential program, and one of the things that they drilled into our heads was being facilitators in the classroom, so I went in and "facilitated" the class. Students weren't used to that kind of instruction; they were used to "you give us information we regurgitate it." I kept pushing them, and the more pushing I did, the more pushback I would get. Students were frustrated because they thought that I wasn't teaching them. I wanted them to do the science experiments, but I wanted them to personalize the experience. Then the Vice Principal got on me, and I remember a parent came in upset because her student wasn't getting A's in the class; he was getting an 88% in a high-level science class. The Vice Principal told the parent that I was having challenges with my planning, and I felt totally stabbed in the back by that comment.

So, I kept pushing forward and said I was going to continue "facilitating" instruction. Maybe I was a bit more stubborn than I should have been. Maybe I should have given in and gone to direct instruction, but this is really what my students needed, to be able to process information and create their own learning. And had this been now, today, I would have been totally on the personalized learning wavelength.

At the end of that year, I remember there was a big argument in class, and one student was like, "You know what? Ntoya's right! We should be able to learn this on our own, but we can't. What does that mean? We're supposed to be the honors kids and supposed to be able to create our own learning, but we can't. And whenever he gives us a problem, we complain, and we moan, and we can't get it done. Why not?"

He totally stuck up for me, and little by little other students would come to tell me that they really appreciated the approach. But it was a battle.

The lesson that I learned from that was to stick with your gut. You are the professional in the classroom, and you know what's good for your students. As long as you are student-centered and put the students first, everything you try is going to be successful, because it's about the students. It wasn't about me, and not about administration. It was about students learning science and being able to apply their learning in real situations.

SHARE: AN UNSCRIPTED PLAN THAT WENT BETTER THAN YOU THOUGHT.

#QUOTES4EDU

MY FRIENDSHIP WITH DENNIS

In my own experience of years of being separated into different tracks in school, I recall students feeling that they couldn't go to college because they were in the "business track." The students in the "college track" didn't feel like they would have the skills to run a business or know how to take care of daily family activities. As students, we believed we were defined by our track, which determined our ability.

Dennis Griffin is an amazing educator and his passion for education is contagious. I am fortunate to have connected with Dennis through Twitter and then as a member of the Edugladiators Core Warriors. We had the chance to finally meet in person at the Summer Spark conference in 2018 and I had the opportunity to see him present in 2019. Dennis is truly an exceptional educator and I am thankful to call him my friend.

Chapter 12

THE LIES THAT STUDENTS BELIEVE

DENNIS GRIFFIN JR.

"Often the labels kids receive become the lies that they believe."

— *Scott Barry Kaufman*

Our world is predicated on labels. If you do not believe me, take a second and describe a person, place, or thing. How do you think someone else would describe the same person, place, or thing? Did anything stick out to you? The adjectives that we teach kids to utilize to enhance the imagery of our writing and our minds become the labels of our future. Labels have the power to define or try to provide context to the world in which we live. Labels make people feel safe. When people can define a person, place, thing, or phenomenon through their verbal or written language, they can rationalize it. The rationale fits within their schema, leaving them with a sense of security. When people encounter a situation that does not fit into their schema, it creates fear and as Andrew Smith stated, "people fear what they do not understand." Jost & Hunyady's (2003) idea of system justification indicates that people who are most afflicted by the status quo (which reinforces labels) would attempt to rationalize that this is the way life is intended to be, and therefore are reluctant to question, let alone try to change the system. Ask yourself: What impact does system justification have on the world of education?

Labels are probably more prevalent in the world of education than anywhere else. If you do not believe me, think about how we label our schools: urban, rural, suburban, high-performing, or low-performing. Each label places a different image of the school in your mind. Think about how we label our student's academic abilities: high, medium, or low. Just imagine how you would feel if you were labeled as a low reader, defined by disability, or the zip code that your school is in. The phenomena that I am referring to are the Pygmalion and Golem Effects. The Golem Effect is the phenomenon when lower expectations are placed on a person and lead to negative results. Compared with The Pygmalion Effect, where high expectations yield high results, both start with what we believe about others. What we think about others directly influences our actions towards others. Our actions, in turn, affect the beliefs that people have about themselves. Finally, the person's beliefs about themselves directly impact their actions toward us. Before you know it, you are caught in a cycle that can only be changed with a change in our own beliefs. This creates quite the conundrum for educators. We must have the strength of mind and character to see the student for who they currently are and who they will become, rather than succumb to the labels that limit or stunt potential. I am a firm believer that every student has the potential to use their gifts and shine brightly.

When I served as a middle school mathematics educator, I ran into a huge problem. Many of my scholars did not want to engage in the learning of higher-level math. They did not want to come to the board and explain their thinking to their classmates. I tried to make the lessons more engaging. I decided to personalize the lessons more. I would even have scholars explain the problem to their group, then freeze up at the thought of going to the board or sharing their solution with the rest of the class. It was not the board that made my scholars stop cold in their tracks. It was the labels their peers would give them for being right or wrong, for being smart or not. Once I identified this problem, the only solution I had was to enhance the view I possessed of my scholars' abilities and make it visible and audible for the world to know. I implemented an expectation that right or wrong, we applauded everyone that went to the board. My actions and perceptions served as the number one determinant in the change that occurred in our culture of learning. It was something that I had complete control over. Do not get me wrong; there were times where I had doubts and allowed fear to creep into my mind. I had times when I was talking to my colleagues, and I was ready to embrace the label that was placed upon someone else. Honestly, it probably would have been easier to accept the label. However, I did not enter this profession for it to be easy. I joined this profession to plant a seed that makes a difference for a young person's tomorrow. The option to not try was taken away. The opportunity to give up did not exist. The option was, "I am here to ensure you learn at high levels because I believe in who you are becoming, not the label that was placed upon you."

To this day, I have yet to meet a student that did not want to demonstrate their talents by being in front of the class. What happens is that fear sets in and the potential to be labeled makes them lose their way. However, the impact of that label continues to grow within them and will manifest when they become adults. As educators, we must ask ourselves a few questions if we want to change the trajectory of our students:

- What was the learning experience of our students before they had me?
- What do we want the future outcomes of our students to be?

- Where is my entry point to begin to deconstruct the labels for that student?
- What seed will I plant and allow others to help me nourish?
- Do I believe in this student?
- If I do not believe, how do I change my mindset to counteract the label that will determine how this student will potentially see themselves?

These questions can only be answered through a transparent process of self-reflection, where we decide to be the agent of change and the source of hope for our students.

Labels tend to stop individuals from taking risks. Carol Dweck (2008) speaks of this in her work that focuses on growth mindset. Being classified as the "smart student" often left me dreading being wrong in front of my peers and teachers. There was even a time that if I was not in the top tier of students in my class, I felt defeated. Powell & Koltz (2012) warn everyone not to let your ego and your position become so connected that when you lose your position, you lose your ego. When I lost my label, my self-identity and self-worth suffered. Fortunately, I was one of the lucky ones. I had a support system around me that helped pull me through that rough patch of my life. My support system included caring parents, educators, and friends. I know I can ensure that every student whose path I cross has a caring adult in their corner to support them through the tough times.

Another element to labels is that they validate generalizations that perpetuate bias and enhance stereotypes. The generalizations and stereotypes are spread through various media outlets often without being fact-checked for credibility. The result is that we have championed those that have risen above the labels that were placed upon them, and deservingly so. The question that I have is, why did we find this to be a shocking feat? Is everyone celebrating the achievement, or are we celebrating the fact that someone accomplished what we deemed impossible for them based on the confines of our abilities and minds?

As a society, we decided to lower an expectation for our members. Therefore, when they excel, we believe that they have become an exception when the reality is their accomplishment should be the norm. I can tell you what I celebrate in these situations. I celebrate the fact that they had the fortitude, perseverance, self-efficacy, and belief in themselves to not be denied and to not allow anyone to give them a standing based on a label. I celebrate that they have now inspired others to fight the labels that have been placed upon them. I rejoice that one day someone will look at them and say, because of you I am who I am today.

DENNIS GRIFFIN JR. serves as an elementary principal in Wisconsin. He has seven years of experience as a middle school educator and is in his fifth year as an administrator. He is currently pursuing his doctoral studies in Educational Leadership at Cardinal Stritch University. Dennis believes all students will be successful in school when they develop relationships with educators that value their gifts, cultures, and individuality.

Chapter 13

PUSHING THE LIMITS: PERSISTENCE, RESILIENCE, AND TENACITY

"What would life be if we had no courage to attempt anything?"

— *Vincent Van Gogh*

W hen I used to think about teaching, I had an image in mind of what a classroom and a teacher "should" look like. Whether it developed from having been a student for many years, identifying with a specific teacher and their methods, or something that I learned from TV shows and movies I had seen, there was a "model teacher" and a "model classroom" that I imagined. I developed a teacher persona that I feel like I have to live up to all the time. When I first started teaching, I thought I had to always follow my exact lesson plan, assign homework every night, give tests every week, and talk throughout the whole class period. Beginning on day one of each new school year and continuing to the last day, everything had a routine. No room for flexibility or student choices because I thought that these were not options. I can still hear myself saying to the students, "You will have homework every single night and even over a holiday break." I cannot even believe that I thought and said that, let alone had that as part of my practice. However, it is the way that I had been taught, and quite honestly, thought it was what I had to do in my own classroom. As though learning would only happen if students were constantly "engaged" in some activity, whether it was listening to me, taking notes, completing a worksheet, starting homework, or working on a project. It took years for me to realize that I could break away from the mold that I had poured myself into and reconfigure the teacher "model" that I thought I had to fit, because what I had been doing wasn't working. I thought that I was creating this awesome environment for my students, that they enjoyed being there and were engaged, but I had completely misinterpreted the "look" of my classroom and had no idea of what true engagement meant.

As educators, we need to be the ones who make a difference. We need to take some risks, and instead of focusing first on the content, we need to start by thinking about the students we teach and the environment we are creating with them.

"Be creative. Use unconventional thinking. And have the guts to carry it out." — *Lee Iacocca*

Jennifer Ledford
6th grade ELA teacher
Indiana
@MrsLedford6Eng

To me, this quote is at the heart of education. Creativity can indeed be complicated. Many believe they do not have it and will never achieve the magic that a creative spirit seems to bring. Yet much like exercising, creativity is a muscle. It must be stretched to reach its potential.

In my first project of the school year, I said to my students, "Display your memoir in whatever creative way you wish." This scared many of them. They wanted guidelines. They wanted explanations. What they didn't know is that in doing this, I was developing a creative culture, an environment that encouraged them to think out of the "norms" of school. It was a scary move for me to develop a project such as this, yet as stated in the quote, I had the guts to carry it out. Sure, many of them stuck to the safety of a slides presentation, but some took the risk and developed raps, plays, or dioramas. By the time the second project came around (a project that was much more structured), I found that more students were asking about options that were not on my choice board. Some teachers would be scared by this. Not me. I embrace this creative culture and all the wonder it provides for my students.

"Personal growth is not a matter of learning new information but of unlearning old limits." — *Alan Cohen*

Melissa Pilakowksi
@mpilakow

When I started teaching, I looked to other teachers for how I "should be" in the classroom. One workshop instructor taught me to be very explicit with rules, expectations, and time. "Don't waste a second," they said.

So, I eschewed every fun and extraneous activity, such as the "Celebrate Life" activity I used to do to start every class, where students shared the positive in their lives. When students asked me why I stopped, I said, "There just isn't enough time."

Later, when I had a year of very challenging students, I'd ask myself "What would Ms. _____ do?" If a student talked back, I'd get in their face. I'd try to confront every off-task behavior, every minute infraction, and curb it immediately, all because that was what was expected of me as a "good" teacher.

Then I joined Twitter, and it's not hyperbole to say that connecting with other educators changed my teaching. Call it cliché, but I call it real.

Expanding my network of colleagues opened my world. Until then, I'd been limited to seeing and hearing what my local colleagues did in their classrooms. I compared myself with them, strove to be more like them.

Twitter introduced me to hundreds, then thousands of other teachers who used different methods with different approaches. They challenged my thinking about assessments, room design, student choice and input, and most of all, relationships.

I brought back the "Celebrate Life" board to build relationships. I moved to blended learning and added a couch. When students get off task, I strike up a conversation with them rather than reprimanding them. Most of all, I stopped thinking about how other teachers would approach a situation; instead, I did what I felt was best for that student at that moment.

My PLN on Twitter helped me grow. I realized I didn't need new lessons, tech tools, or classroom management techniques. I needed to be open to my students and give them voice and choice. I needed to build relationships. I needed to enjoy my students and learn with them rather than teach at them.

Once I figured this out, I wasn't limited to being like other teachers. I could be my own innovative, one-of-a-kind teacher.

And that's something worth putting on our "Celebrate Life" board tomorrow.

———

AT THE END of each day, when we reflect on our classes and the work we did, a large part of what we think of should be the interactions we had with our students. What did we do to make learning better or different for them, and what did we learn from them that will help us to be better tomorrow? There is always room to grow, and even when we experience failures, we can't give up. We just have a new starting point.

Every great story 📖
🌍 on the planet
happened when someone
decided not to give up,
but kept going no matter what.
-Spryte Loriano

Tisha Richmond

"Every great story on the planet happened when someone decided not to give up, but kept going no matter what." — Spryte Loriano

---

We have all been there. Facing a challenge, sometimes unexpected, a bump in the road that makes us want to give in, call it a day and move on. I know personally, there have been many times where I did give up and never looked back again. But there have also been times I gave up, but only briefly. I recharged, went back and tried twice as hard the next time. I've had my share of challenges and frustrations like everyone else, and what makes it different for me is that as an educator, I am not supposed to give up. I can't. What kind of a role model would I be if I cowered in the face of difficulty and walked away from a challenge?

I'm sure we all have students who tell us they "can't do" something, or they "won't be good at it," or they say they're flat out not doing it. I hear it every day, multiple times. Do we let them get away with that? Should we? Our students count on us to lead them, and if they see us giving up when we come up against a challenge, that is not the example we should set for them. It tells them it's okay if you give something a try and it doesn't work then give up and move on. But we need to do more than that. By taking a risk, even if it's something that you feel is so far out of your range of possibilities and capabilities, you show you are not afraid to fail. Putting yourself out there and taking that chance even one time is far better than the alternative, never trying and then later wondering what might have been.

"It's not about the destination; it's about the journey."

— Ralph Waldo Emerson, American Essayist

We hear stories all the time of people who focus on perseverance, resilience, and failing forward. We can think about people throughout history who persevered through failures to bring about different changes to the world, whether in education, business, technology, or medicine, as a few examples. They kept going in spite of the odds that might have continued to stack up against them. We must do the same.

Heather Lippert
Kindergarten Teacher
Cedar Valley Community School
@msyoung114

The year had been filled with negative feedback. I cried in my classroom regularly. Every evaluation held words about why I shouldn't be a teacher, that I wasn't good enough. Then word came — my contract would not be renewed, and I was let go from my teaching position. I failed. I found a choice: give up and leave the career that was my calling, a dream I held since childhood, or take the risk and apply for jobs with my non-renewal. I closed my eyes and jumped. I filled out the applications with the negative feedback nipping at my brain.

I was hired. September came, and I found myself in a job share position with two teachers, who said they knew in the first five minutes of my interview that I was their match. The following year I was hired into a fantastic school. Six years later I'm still thriving and growing in those walls. Last year I became a National Board-Certified Teacher.

There will be those who don't believe in you or your great story, but you are the writer, and your push (no matter what) will make your great story come true.

There will always be challenges, some big and some small. We need to share our stories because it's through stories that we connect to find and give strength. And sometimes we can just laugh about some of the crazy experiences that happen in the lives of educators. Every day brings with it opportunities for many things, most of which we can't possibly predict or prepare for ahead of time. We do the best we can with what we have. We keep our heads up and push onward no matter what. Even in what seems like an impossible situation, there is a lesson to be learned, a connection created, and an impact made somewhere in your future. We just may not realize it...yet. Even those situations that might feel like the worst we have gone through might end up teaching us the most valuable lesson or opening a door in a new direction.

I love having friends like Toutoule, who help me to brainstorm strategies to engage my students more in learning. He gives excellent advice, pushes my thoughts, and has fantastic stories to share. I tried to recreate this story that Toutoule told me, in his voice, and this might be my favorite of all time.

Dr. Toutoule Ntoya
Instructional Coach
Pasadena, CA
@toutoulentoya
www.toutoulentoya.com

I took a job at a brand-new school. We had a team together, and we were really excited about getting started. I started the year in a closet, literally a closet. The closet probably held 10-12 students. One day when class was over, all of the kids left the closet, and two of the boys in the class got into it. One boy said something to the other boy, the other boy stared him down, then they started to push each other, which then turned into a big wrestling match in the closet. I had to break up a fight in the closet.

So, I was moved out of the closet and into a hallway. It was a "classroom," but the classroom had no doors, and it was the main entry to the main office. So, you can imagine what parents thought when they came to the school, and they had to walk through it in order to get into the main office. One time a kid got in a fight in someone else's class, and they had to walk him through *my* classroom on the way to the office. He stopped and had a conversation with my whole class about how he had gotten into a fight with another student, how it was "cool" because he won, and then they escorted him into the office.

It was the best and the worst experience of my teaching career. Hilarious. It was not the kids either, it was the circumstances, the lack of support, the lack of resources, but we made it work. We were all in it together, all of us.

I think the lesson I learned was the importance of flexibility. It wasn't the best or even ideal environment, but I had to make it work. My students and I bonded around our classroom being a closet. Being flexible and being able to connect with my students made the difference.

There were growing pains. It was only the second year for the school, all of us trying to figure it out. Some days were good and others not so good. We had created a culture because of our time together, and we made a connection. And I'm not sure if I've ever made a connection as close as I did with that group of students.

It was all about our collective culture, connecting with students, and being flexible. Nothing is ever perfect, but you have to learn how to deal with everything in its imperfection.

Nothing is ever perfect,

but you have to learn

how to deal with

everything in its

imperfection.

DR. TOUTOULE NTOYA

#QUOTES4EDU

I can relate to Toutoule's story because I didn't have my own class-room for a few years and the environment was less than ideal. I was teaching in a computer lab (a small room off of the library), and also a classroom with no doors. Toutoule's story definitely resonated with me. While we all hope to not have a similar "class-room" experience, there are lessons we can learn from what he shared.

Remember to stay focused on our true purpose. It's not always about where we learn; it's about the climate and culture we create and what we do in that learning space. We have to be flexible, and sometimes that means adapting to situations that are beyond our control, like dealing with interruptions, changes in routines, and unpredictable events. By staying positive and keeping our humor, we can form a bond with our students. What a way to work on social-emotional learning skills as well as being adaptable to unique situations that can pop up in classrooms.

"There is no greater agony than bearing an untold story inside of you." — *Maya Angelou*

We learn through the power of storytelling. Sharing our stories gives us an advantage where otherwise we might not have one. We connect, we share vulnerabilities, and this practice can be a source of strength for someone who needs it the most. As educators, we must be prepared for times when the what-ifs and the "impossible" happen. We can't possibly know how to respond to these events without developing a ton of skills along the way. We must think and stretch our comfort zones by taking a risk even when we don't know if we will succeed and aren't guaranteed a positive outcome. Everything we experience is preparation for something else, perhaps another time when our story just might inspire someone to act or offer hope to someone who is ready to give up. In our vulner-abilities and times of weaknesses, we can provide the strength that others need. We must first know ourselves in order to know others and make connections that will help us to grow as professionals and as human beings.

SHARE OUT: HAVE YOU EVER HAD AN EXPERIENCE LIKE TOUTOULE'S? SHARE YOUR STORY.

#QUOTES4EDU

MY FRIENDSHIP WITH HOLLY

I am fortunate to have connected with Holly a few years ago, also through Twitter and engaging in some of the same chats. We have stayed connected through Voxer and I am inspired by her love of teaching and learning. Her passion for education and her positive spirit inspire others to take risks, be vulnerable, and above all, be willing to reflect, grow and stay focused on doing what is best for our students.

Chapter 14

"STEP FORWARD AND GROW, OR STEP BACKWARD IN SAFETY."

HOLLY KING

"Step forward and grow, or step backward in safety."

— Abraham Maslow

As I toured the building of what was soon to be the home of my first high school teaching position, I was introduced to teacher after teacher with 15 or more years of experience. A very young and extremely green educator with little experience besides writing college-mandated six-point lesson plans, I was both curious and envious of these educational veterans: curious about the wisdom that they held after years of experiences, and envious of their tried and true lesson plans that were likely dogeared and worn after so many uses. I envisioned files, organized by topic and in chronological order based on the annual plan, ready to slide from the shelf and move into action. As I looked down, I smiled at my leather portfolio, a gift from my university mentor. Although professional, it only housed additional copies of my resume. Unlike the years of materials that I envisioned these veteran teachers to have, I moved into my classroom with just a notebook and a dream. I hoped that I would, one day, hold the same level of expertise and wisdom. My mind wandered. What would I look like in 20 years? Would I have well-organized binders of intentionally planned and executed lessons, having finally reached the place in my career where I simply needed to turn the page?

In reflection, I realize how lucky I was to learn from these educators during my first few years in the field. This school, 30 years old with only two administrators during that time, was rich in family atmosphere, trust, and collaborative culture. Favors, big and small, were traded without keeping score. We supported one another in our classrooms, on the sports fields, and outside of school. As a brand-new teacher, I was embraced by veteran teachers who tire-lessly offered advice on effective classroom management strategies, writing recommendations, and tips on leading parent conferences. My new teacher friends in other schools were envious of the wisdom that I had at my fingertips, and I eagerly shared my experiences with my network.

The first year was tough. As a science major, I was confident with the knowledge and understanding of the content, however — as you know — teaching the content in an engaging way to ensure mastery requires so much more than simply content knowledge. I poured my heart into developing innovative, engaging lessons that were aligned to standards and provided evidence of mastery. Secretly, I longed for a file cabinet stocked with lessons similar to those that I saw in nearby teachers' classrooms. In fact, I sometimes joked about this with colleagues. However, these veteran teachers whom I admired were quick to remind me that I needed to give myself grace and allow a few years to build a repertoire of plans that included everything from notes to worksheets, and quizzes to tests. I took their advice, persisted, and pushed forward.

Faithful to their wisdom, I documented my lesson plans in detail with copies of every piece of paper used. My unit plans included detailed daily lessons with every warm-up assignment, set of notes, practice worksheet, exit ticket, lab, quiz, project, and test. My lesson plan book became a staple, traveling to and from work with me daily. In fact, it was so thorough that it bordered a work of art. In my brain, it was equally priceless. In this quest to build a teacher library, I remained undeterred.

With piles of papers and eager to replicate the methods of my predecessors, my next step was to organize my materials. After peeking in the classrooms of several teachers who I most admired, I requested hanging files and started to label them. By May, I had two drawers of beautifully organized unit plans ready and eager to begin my second year of teaching. Although this may sound trite, I was proud of my file cabinet and its detailed organization. Not only was this a masterpiece that housed an entire year's worth of educational evidence, but it was also so organized that I envisioned myself teaching by the grab-and-go method in Year #2.

Yet, Year #2 arrived — and the only thing that my files did was gather dust. In preparing for my first unit, I reviewed my previous year's plans realizing that those plans would not work at all — not in year #2 and likely never again. As an educator, I had grown. I was no longer the same teacher that I was when those plans were written. Perhaps there was an activity or two that I could use, however, I found myself rearranging and rewriting so much of my previous years' work that I might as well begin from scratch. Within a week, I also realized that my students had an entirely different set of needs than the previous year, rendering what remained of those two beautiful file drawers, unusable.

Yet, I was persistent in creating that library. All of the veteran teachers had it, so I needed it, too. Right?

I reflected on my lack of use of the files in Year #2, and I found my most obvious flaw to blame: my organizational system did not work. Tossing the files, I decided to switch to binders. By the second spring, I had a bookcase full of neatly labeled binders.

You can guess what happened in Year #3.

Looking back, I tried nearly every organizational tactic known to humanity. I organized these papers into large binders. When that did not work, I tried smaller binders. Still struggling but undeterred from my mission, I utilized a file cabinet in my classroom. I even bought color-coded folders to organize my files.

Regardless of the method to store my instructional materials, I found that a "tried and true" series of lesson plans just did not work for me.

But what didn't work? Certainly, I could find an organizational method for my materials, right? Would I ever reach "Master Teacher" status if I could not even figure out how to organize my materials? What was I doing wrong? Why did I insist on practically recreating my own wheel each and every year?

Although I taught the same subject with the same standards to the same grade level of students, I realized that I needed to make significant adjustments to my plans every single time I taught it. I adjusted the order of units or the topics included within units. I created new activities, laboratory investigations, and experiences to teach or reinforce topics. I edited formative and summative assessments. No two years were alike. Each year, I had grown as an educator. I had knowledge of new instructional strategies, resources, and activities that would enhance the learning experience. More importantly, the students entering my classroom brought different experiences than the students who entered the year before. As we got to know each other, I discovered that my lessons needed to change. And, change they did.

In comparing myself to the veteran teachers in my network, I realized that I was a little bit different. My classroom management style encouraged students to have choice seating long before *flexible seating* was an educational buzzword. I remember one colleague visiting my classroom on a day where the students engaged in a lot of movement. He said, "You'll have them sitting in rows by this time next year! Trust me!" Today, 23 years later, my classroom design still embraces flexible seating. After other similar encounters in areas of assessment, student voice, and the importance of relationships, I confidently realized that it was acceptable to be a different type of teacher than the others. I grew to be comfortable in my own skin, and I sought opportunities that offered research-based support and growth in these very areas

After many years, I finally gave away the dusty file cabinet and all of the unused organization materials that it housed. It was not the binders or file cabinets that failed me. In fact, it was not even the concept of organizing the materials that eluded me. What I could not wrap my brain around was the idea that I could plan a year-long study of a subject by drawing from the knowledge shared by the students in my classroom. Although the traditional nature of this school still prioritized large group lecture-type instruction, I abbreviated lectures and provided more class time for collaborative and supported practice. Two short years later, I flipped my whole-group instruction and used all of the class time to practice together in large groups, small groups, partners, and independently. This seems so obvious now, but, years ago, placing relationships before content in the secondary learning environment was not as mainstream as it is today. This was the beginning of the differentiated instructional model that I continue to use today, a model that I created because it met the needs of the students in my classroom at that given time and space.

In reflection, I realize that the removal of the file cabinet was symbolic, for it illustrated a turning point in my trajectory as an educator.

Although against the grain of veteran teachers in my building, recreating my daily lesson plans each year allowed me to "step forward and grow." Sure, it would have been easier to pull a worksheet from my binder to copy, but it lacked the critical reflection necessary to determine if that, indeed, was the best method for students to illustrate mastery of that particular concept. As the years passed, my students changed as the world surrounded them with opportunities never before available. As an educator determined to produce students who were prepared to face a rapidly changing future, I recognized that the methods of yesteryear would not suffice. Their future successes depended on the ability to critically think, collaborate, creatively problem-solve, and communicate their questions, solutions, and explanations. Not only was it imperative that I teach this way, but I also needed to learn what being a student looks like today.

I immersed myself in alternative 21st-century learning experiences. I said "yes" to every workshop, conference, and professional development opportunity that crossed my desk. With detailed notes and creative energy, I rewrote lessons to integrate new instructional strategies and technology tools into my classrooms. I observed the engagement and investment of my students. I paid close attention to changes in data trends that showed student mastery. I surveyed and interviewed students about the impact of the changes to their learning space.

In a few short months, the language in my science laboratory changed. Students no longer asked, "May I do this...?" Instead, students challenged each other with "Why?" and "What if we did...?" or "What happened to explain these results?" My role significantly changed. No longer was I the just the teacher. Instead, I was a collaborative partner who happened to have a significant amount of content knowledge to steer conversations. However, often, I did not have any more access to the correct answer than the student beside me, particularly when a laboratory investigation did not yield the expected results. Prior to our shift in classroom culture, my students would have whined at another failed lab investigation and dutifully copied the expected results from the board. In a complete hairpin turn, highly-invested students fueled with a desire to understand and produce credible scientific results were not satisfied with a failed laboratory. "Ms. King, we would not just walk away in a real laboratory, so we cannot just walk away here," they reminded me. Who can argue with that logic?

And, so, the transformation took root — in all areas of my educational foundation.

Moving backward, although safe and secure, was not in the best interests of students. Stepping backward allows us to return to our harbor, the place where our ship is safe, the waters are easy to navigate, and we are protected from unknown elements.

Stepping forward was, and continues to be, uncertain. More, stepping forward is uncomfortable. It requires confidence in one's choices and skills. It requires courage to stand up to those who disagree. It requires the bravery to take risky paths that do not always lead to success. It requires the faith to dust off your knees and try again. It requires the willingness to find like-minded educators. And, it requires the vulnerability to lean on these educators for help. My risky strategies were not always admired by my colleagues. On more than one occasion, the teacher across the hall would close my door (not his!) because my students were having entirely too much fun and disrupting his ability to lecture. Colleagues questioned the integrity of my relationships with students, wondering why my classroom was always full at lunch. One teacher even sabotaged my exam reviews by scheduling her mandatory reviews at the same time as my optional ones. With each barrier, I remained flexible with my eye on the goal: student achievement. If I failed to navigate around the barriers being built by those who feared my disruption of the status quo, then I failed the most important part of my job: my students. In the face of adversity, I modeled a positive attitude that focused on solutions, and this framework translated into students adopting this mentality towards challenging coursework.

As I stretched myself professionally, I shared my journey with my students. In exposing my vulnerability in learning new skills, our shared learning space evolved into one that was especially risk-tolerant. Students who never spoke in class talked freely, incorrectly answered questions, and collaboratively solved problems. No longer isolated to established groups, students fluidly moved between groups to ask questions, engage in classroom conversation, and offer assistance. Lawn chairs and bean bags replaced desks; lapboards replaced binders. Seeing the classroom as their canvas of mastery, students wrote on desks with chalk markers, created elaborate murals the length of the wall to illustrate connections among multiple units of study, and collaborated on podcasts in lieu of traditional lab reports.

Thankfully, throughout this professional transition, I worked under the leadership of a forward-thinking principal who believed in giving teachers full autonomy in their classrooms. Our meetings about my teaching performance were interesting, He once told me that he never saw me actually "teaching," but the students in my classroom were always on-task. He said, "You know, I can't put my finger on what you are doing or how you are pulling it off, but the students are running to your classroom. They grab their lunch and return to your room. Whatever you are doing, keep doing it." What I was doing was fostering creativity, risk-taking, failing forward, trust, and vulnerability; encouraging collaboration, critical thinking, and creativity; building student leadership capacity, and helping students learn how to use their voice in today's world. To keep doing it was exactly what I did.

The transition that I described to you happened during my 17th year as an educator. With nearly 20 years under my belt, the easier path would have been the one explained to me by my mentors. That path would have included a playbook of lessons, ready for the next group of students each year. Yet, that felt stagnant, unchallenged, and shallow. My students clearly articulated the educational environment that they needed to thrive. Once their eyes were opened, we could not turn back.

Tomorrow's world leaders require innovative practices. They demand opportunities to collaboratively solve real problems and authentically use their voices to globally communicate. We have resources to integrate these opportunities into the classroom, and it is professional malpractice to provide anything less than the very best education for every student who crosses our door.

Since this story, I have moved to another district, but still remain very close with the educators who mentored me during my early years, namely my assigned mentor. In learning of her upcoming retirement, I paid her a visit during the week that she happened to be cleaning out her classroom for the teacher who would be assuming her teaching responsibilities. This teacher is a brilliant educator. Single-handedly, I learned more from my conversations with her than any other resource, course, or text during my educational career. Watching her pack her classroom brought tears to my eyes as I knew that her wisdom was leaving with her on that very day. As we packed up her things, she found a file drawer of unit lessons and started to go through the first one. My mind returned to the first time we met, and our conversations about the value of building a teacher resource library. With no way of knowing the flashback in my mind, she looked at me with a twinkle in her eye and said, "You know, I don't even know why I kept the files for the last few years. It isn't like I have looked at them in years."

I held my laughter. Little did I know how parallel our journeys were. My mentor and idol, with children my age, and me, fresh out of graduate school — saving files, but rarely touching them. Recreating lessons despite a culture that says otherwise. Two educators, changing our practices just as quickly as the students in front of us change. Two educators, comfortable with being uncomfortable.

Stepping forward remains uncomfortable and uncertain. But, stepping forward is the only way that we (and our students) will grow.

HOLLY IS A VETERAN SCIENCE EDUCATOR, *a champion of integrating technologies in the educational setting, and an avid risk taker with respect to transforming learning spaces through collaboration, personalized professional development, and individual goal setting. When not teaching, you can find her paddle boarding, spearfishing, or saving sea turtles in her home in the Outer Banks of North Carolina. Connect with her on Twitter @hollysking.*

Chapter 15

SEEING THE STUDENT

"Empathy is a choice; it's a vulnerable choice. In order to connect with you, I have to connect with something within myself that knows that feeling." — *Brené Brown*

T eaching requires more than knowing and becoming masters of the content. We need to understand our students and be observant to more than just who they are and their needs when it comes to learning. We need to be aware of what each student is bringing to the classroom. What we "see" when they walk into the room is not necessarily a clear picture of who they are nor can it provide us with a good understanding about their life beyond the time spent in our classroom or in our school. We can only form this connection if we are intentional about building those relationships. We need to foster connections with our students and their families, so we understand their backgrounds, their learning experiences, and who they are.

"People's behavior makes sense if you think about it in terms of their goals, needs, and motives." — *Thomas Mann*

Paul O'Neill
Supervisor of Instruction
@pauloneill1972

Earlier in my career, I worked exclusively with students who were classified with profound disabilities. I worked diligently to find strategies to improve student behavior. It took many years of experience and reflection to realize that behavior is a form of communication. Sometimes, students are unable to use words to express themselves. Instead of trying to find universal strategies to address behavior, my focus became supporting the individual. I began focusing my effort and energy on the *needs* of each individual as opposed to focusing on the *performance* of the individual. Truly knowing a student and understanding them helped me to support individuals instead of addressing their behaviors. This revelation changed my whole approach and led to an unprecedented level of growth and development in student achievement.

As Paul's experience shows, if we are only looking at the class as a whole and not learning about individual needs, whether for learning or behavior, then we are doing students a disservice. Students go through a lot, and we don't always know about the good and the bad, but we need to prioritize learning as much as we can about them and what, if any, challenges they might be facing. We must be able to identify signs that they need help, not just in our class, but in dealing with life in general. Students can become lost in a world full of choices, challenges, and changes, and they are counting on us to help them develop the skills to pursue their dreams and persevere.

"You can't go back and change the beginning, but you can start where you are and change the ending." — C.S. Lewis

---

I've never really liked discipline. Not as a child, not as a student, and not as a teacher. It was always a struggle for me to deal with adverse student behaviors because I believed that "yelling" meant that I was a mean teacher, and I don't have it in me to be mean. I don't want to be. I remember being yelled at when I was in school. It did not happen often, but regardless of who was getting yelled at, it made me feel awful and made me not want to be in class. In my own teaching experience with 22 years in my school, there have been less than 10 times where I would say that I have "lost it" and yelled. I've actually been ashamed of my responses and reactions to some student behaviors because I just didn't know how to process it and handled it poorly. Instead of being angry, I yelled. As the adult, it was in my power to do different, to think before speaking, but sometimes the anger and frustration won out.

Not my Proudest Moments: Memories and Lessons Learned

Early in my career, there was a shouting match that spanned the length of a hallway; students parted to the sides and just watched, afraid to move. At one end was a student and at the other, me. An argument which started because of sports ineligibility due to grades. I did not handle it well —I was trying to save face as a new teacher, and I was losing.

There was also the time in a study hall when a ninth-grade student stood up and yelled at me in front of a cafeteria full of students because I had assigned seats. I pushed back just as hard and did not back down. It was uncomfortable, made me feel awful, and bothered me for days. It also happened in front of a cafeteria full of students, many of whom I taught.

There was the time I was repeatedly interrupted in class by random noises, comments, singing, and sometimes banging on the desks. Occasionally students would engage in an argument with a peer and I would quickly lose the attention of the class. When I tried to handle the distraction, other students would start something new, and I had to stop class again. Sometimes wishing to avoid discipline referrals, I was patiently redirecting, trying to make it through, only to get to the last five minutes when frustration (then anger) took over. I lost it and immersed the whole class in that negativity. I'm sure this left an imprint on their minds of a different side of me, one that I was not proud of that day, or the days that followed.

There have been times that students exchanged words in class, sometimes discretely and many times breaking into a yelling and insult-filled disruption that involved the whole class. I struggled, yelled, lost composure, and was not at my best.

And there were times, weeks and months later, that students called me out on my "lack of intervention" during class. I was challenged because I did not take action quickly enough to deal with an argument that erupted in class. I tried to do the best that I could, but I could have done better.

Give Yourself Grace

A few of these stories are similar, but there was something different about the last two experiences. I took time to apologize, to openly discuss, and also to give myself a bit of grace. In those conversations, the students told me that it was "okay." I responded that no, it was not. I was sorry that I reacted the way that I did, and I wanted to make sure that they knew it. We must admit when we are wrong, and also give ourselves grace. We do the best we can until we know better. If we don't, we will lose the power of reflection and of becoming a better version of ourselves. For me, giving myself grace means that I forgive myself for not handling a situation better, invest in improving and be intentional about apologizing when I need to, when I am wrong.

"The best thing about being a teacher is that it matters. The hardest thing about being a teacher is that it matters every day."

— *Todd Whitaker*

With the stories I shared, you might think that relationships were damaged, if they existed at all. Or perhaps that I avoided the student or maybe treated them differently. None of the above. The study hall student took my class the next year, and it was a talking point that led to a positive and supportive connection. Each of those "interactions" somehow ended up being the way we connected and started to build a more solid, supportive relationship, one that lasted beyond the time we spent in school. I had them as students and now know them as friends.

These students are well into their mid- to late-30s, successful, with families and the knowledge that there are teachers out there that will do whatever it takes to make a difference. I want to be that teacher — admit when I am wrong, strive to be better, and work to see the student first, and not the behavior.

It is not always a student that presents challenges like these. About 12 years ago, I was confronted by a colleague about a "look" I gave during lunch. I was called "high and mighty," insulted about my appearance, and screamed at in front of many students and teachers. I did not see this interaction coming. It took me by surprise because I don't even remember the lunch conversation. Disagreements, I can handle, but ones which are one-sided and take place in a hallway full of students, I cannot. But I kept my composure, and even though the words hurt, and others heard them, I did not push back. I only asked, "why?"

Did I appear weak to others? To this colleague, yes. Students? Maybe. But I did not want them to remember or hear something that I could not take away — something that could impact how they viewed me as a teacher, and their comfort in my classroom. Hard to see it this way, but I was still in control. I could handle my reactions and responses. Even when we don't think they can hear us or see our interactions, students are watching. My inner voice reminds me to never say things that I cannot take back. No insults, no harsh words...simply keep as composed as I can, be patient, and let it pass. No matter what someone says to me, my response is and will always be kindness.

I've tried to improve, but sometimes I catch myself reacting to the behavior first and not seeing the student, not understanding what the cause might be. That's not something that I realized until one Friday afternoon, when I noticed something that left me feeling happy, sad, and just different. I will tell you more about it a bit later.

"Each mistake teaches you something new about yourself. There is no failure, remember, except in no longer trying. It is the courage to continue that counts." – Chris Bradford

---

Years passed without any real behavioral issues, and I became used to not having to deal with discipline referrals or situations like those of my early years. However, I started to experience more challenges with student behaviors the past two years, and some days it was difficult to get through the class period. As soon as I would get one situation somewhat under control, another one would pop up. The behaviors were causing serious disruptions, an uncomfortable environment for learning and left the students and myself not feeling too great about class. Learning became difficult with the disruptions. It left me feeling frustrated and unsure of what to do. When thinking about it, I could not believe some of the behaviors that were happening in my class: noises, students talking over me, and making unkind comments to class-mates. I tried not to yell, but there were times that my patience escaped and was replaced by frustration that I could not keep inside.

It helps when you know the whole story or at least enough of it so you understand the lens you must look through to get a better "view." If we don't have the right "lens" and we lack information to filter through to really understand our students and their needs, we will lose opportunities to provide a more personalized and inten-tional learning experience for them.

Over the years, I've overheard some of the following "concerns" from teachers: "What's wrong with them? Why can't they just...? What am I supposed to do with them? Why are they so bad? Why won't they work? Do they even study anymore? How can I get them to do their homework? They can't figure it out, there is no effort!" These remarks surprised me because as educators, and professionals, we must keep our minds free of judgment. These "concerns" all referred to behavioral issues, student apathy, and attitudes toward learning. As educators, how can we respond without knowing if there's more to the story? What lens are we using when asking these questions and making these comments? Do we see all students as the same? Are we just seeing the behavior that is interfering with *us* or is it interfering with student learning? What assumptions are we making about students, whether voicing them or just in our actions?

Does it make a difference? Yes, I believe that it does. We need to address and stop behaviors that interfere with student learning, but when it comes to behaviors that directly impact us, I think we need to look more closely. We can't make it personal.

Did a student interrupt me in order to ask a question, or did they lean over to ask a classmate for something? Are these behavioral issues? Maybe. We have a tough decision to make, especially in deciding how we handle the situation. Do we involve the whole class and further disrupt, or do we find a way to connect with the student? It has taken years of practice, of making mistakes and then reflecting, to realize that I had not always handled interruptions or student behaviors well. At times overreacting, when instead I could have paused before speaking, or spoke in soft words directly to the student. Our words matter and we don't know the impact they will have on students long after they leave our classrooms, so we must actively reflect on how we handle these situations and how to keep doing better.

"Sometimes a simple, almost insignificant gesture on the part of a teacher can have a profound formative effect on the life of a student."
— *Paulo Freire, Pedagogy of Freedom*

Sarah Fromhold
Digital Learning Coach
Frisco ISD
@sew1080

Getting your class roster is something teachers wait for with anticipation. As I opened my roster for the first time in a new school, 16 fresh, new names and faces greeted me.

I showed my list to my team and received warnings about one boy in particular. "Watch out for Joseph*! He will destroy your room when he gets angry." If I'm being honest, I was scared when Joseph walked into my room on the first day of school. What if I set him off? What if I can't calm him down?

During our first spelling test of the year, I could see him becoming more and more frustrated. I leaned down beside him and whispered that we could finish on our own later in the day.

As the weeks went by, I made it a point to get to know Joseph on a deeper level. I found out his parents were recently divorced, his dad was recently diagnosed with cancer, and he was resentful at the cards life had dealt him. Throughout our year together, he took risks that I don't think would have happened without first building trust. He pushed himself to learn more with his classmates and me because my room was a safe space for him.

In March of that year, we had a college basketball team visit the school. Their coach talked to the students about the importance of listening to their teachers. He told them that teachers had their best interests at heart. The second those words were spoken, Joseph looked straight at me. I gave him a little wink, and he smiled the biggest smile back at me.

That small act of getting on his level during that first spelling test formed a fast bond between the two of us. I was sad to leave Joseph when summer came. I was moving to a different position within the district, and I hoped Joseph would continue the new path he had forged for himself. I saw him recently, now a fifth grader, and he immediately gave me a big hug. We chatted and I found out his dad is cancer-free, and Joseph is excited to move on to middle school.

Joseph will always have a special place in my heart, and I will always think of him fondly.

(Name changed to protect the privacy of the student.)

"A good teacher must be able to put himself in the place of those who find learning hard." — Eliphas Levi

---

A good teacher must be able
to put himself in the place of
those who find learning hard.
~ Eliphas Levi, French Author

@fishrich

How many times have teachers been told stories about students that will be coming to their classroom, whether at the start of the year or in the middle of the year? I'm sure many have been warned about *that* class or *that* student or given tips on how to place students in the classroom. While part of me understands how it might be helpful, I know that it can also be harmful. How many times have you warned others? I had shared stories, but they were from years ago, and I have tried to know just enough about each student to provide the best experience and support that I can for them. Knowing enough means I am aware of any special accommodations that might be needed, have access to family and health information, and most importantly, I spend time getting to know them. I don't want to know about all of their "history" in other classes, not entirely, because I don't want a clouded view of them to start before they can show me who they are. I want to see each student through my own lens.

My own recent experiences served as a reminder to *see the student*. I heard stories and read notes about "Student A," and I was concerned. It put me on guard more than I might have been. Without sharing specific details and to maintain privacy, the only thing I can say is that on one Friday afternoon, I truly *saw* the student for the first time. I saw who the student was, and not their behavior. For the first time, I was asked (by student A) to help him finish a task, a simple word search. I saw persistence, engagement, curiosity, and a genuine interest in learning more. We discussed the words (there was even laughter), and in the end, we had a short conversation about how fun it was to do the word search. We both said, "have a good weekend," and that was the last day Student A was in my class. I was happy, surprised, and sad all at the same time. I wondered if that student had "been there" all along, and I had only been looking through the lens of behavior. Did I place a limit on Student A's learning by focusing on what the data said, rather than judging for myself? And rather than letting him show me? Seeing the student means knowing them, who they are, what they are interested in, and how to reach them for learning. No assumptions, just observations.

"A child is only as disabled as their environment and the beliefs of the people around them." — Bala Pillai DPT, PCS

Marialice B.F.X. Curran, Ph.D.
Founder & Executive Director
Digital Citizenship Institute
Connecticut
@mbfxc

One of my favorite memories in the classroom happened in the EagleEyes classroom at the Campus School at Boston College. EagleEyes is assistive technology that was created at Boston College over 20 years ago to help people with severe physical disabilities who cannot speak and can move only their eyes or head. Eye movement replaces the mouse, and the eyes control the cursor and clicks by eye movement.

Over the years, I witnessed a lot of assumptions about students who were nonverbal and nonambulatory. One student, in particular, set the record straight during his annual IEP when the school district came to observe an EagleEyes session. Offline, the school district held up flash-cards of numbers and asked him to give an eyes up for the higher number. The school personnel held up numbers like five and seven, and kept asking the student to pick the highest number. With no eye movement, the student had a firm "no" face on as he refused to answer the question.

Once set up on the EagleEyes system, with his eyes, the student gazed at individual letters to spell out a message: You insult me.

This was a defining moment for me as an educator and as a

learner. Every single one of our students come to our class-rooms with individual gifts and talents, and it's really up to us to bring out the very best in each of them.

"When you have a disability, knowing that you are not defined by it is the sweetest feeling." — Anne Wafula Strike

---

I asked Marialice about some of her experiences. She shared a few with me, and when I heard this story, I knew it had to be told. A few years ago, I heard a young woman speak about her hopes and dreams for the future. Her speech was done through the use of an augmentative and alternative communication (AAC) device. She had to push against the head cushion to move the cursor on the Dynavox screen when she either spelled or selected words as she spoke. She was brilliant, funny, brave, and an inspiration. She shared an important message that day. Don't make assumptions about the abilities of students. Give them a chance, they can do amazing things. Just wait and see.

"Be mindful when it comes to your words. A string of some that don't mean much to you may stick with someone for a lifetime."

— Rachel Wolchin

Paul O'Neill
Supervisor of Instruction
@pauloneill1972

I'll never forget this story told to me by a colleague. Mr. "Smith* said he had joked with this student all year long. The two had a great rapport and enjoyed laughing together often, but today something was different. Mr. Smith read an essay submitted by Billy* and said to him, "Come on! Don't take the lazy way, I know you can do better." The teacher looked up at the student who was red-faced and had just uttered a profanity. The teacher was speechless as Billy stormed out of the room. Mr. Smith felt terrible. While he meant no harm, his choice of words had hurt the feelings of one of his students. Billy went to the office to see a counselor. As he tried to regain his composure, Billy mentioned that his father had often called him lazy. What Mr. Smith did not know was that Billy had an estranged relationship with his father. Hearing the word "lazy" resulted in the flood of memories that caused Billy to reflect back on some painful moments from his past. This story provided a powerful reminder for Mr. Smith and his colleagues.

Paul's story reinforces the importance of knowing our students and where they come from. We all have bad days and sometimes when our students act out, it's because they are dealing with something happening within our classroom, or they might be going through something at home. It is our responsibility to find out how we can help and support them. We may not want to pry, but to truly do what is best for our students, we need to be a source of comfort for them. We care about the "whole child," and some may say that's not part of the "job," but it is. Our job is not limited to the hours of the school day or to the moments that we spend with each student in our class. We need to be accessible to our students even after they leave our classrooms.

"The value of nothing? Out of nothing, comes something."

— *Amy Tan*

Matthew Larson
Vice Principal
Millville Public Charter School
Millville, NJ
@mlarson_nj

"What do you mean he won't be getting a letter grade?"

"Well, he will still be getting a letter grade...P, G, S, S+."

This class was going to add 0 points to my GPA. That's right. Zero.

This was a conversation between my mother and my new English language arts teacher as I began my seventh-grade year, newly-minted as an honors student. They were discussing the grading system that our teacher used which was drastically different than the traditional 0 to 100, A-F format I had gotten really good at attaining.

"How is he supposed to know how he is doing?"

"Don't worry. He will know."

Not only did I complete the seventh and eighth grade knowing how I was doing in ELA — I came out learning and doing everything much better. You see, this class was all about individualized feedback. In this class, we did creative writing with oral presentation, research papers, skits in front of our peers, and research projects that had to be presented in front of the class for a minimum of 15 minutes. Each and every assignment was accompanied by handwritten annotations and specific feedback to the student.

"Too many verbal fillers: um, you know, like;" "Fidgeting

too much with hands, use them for gestures;" "Walk the room, don't sway side-to-side and turn your feet over;" "Project more, more vocal inflections."

The feedback was real. The feedback was authentic. The feedback was not judgmental but informative. The feedback gave me the opportunity to learn specifically what I needed to do better in order to improve.

The goal was not to chase some letter or number for a grade. The goal was not to boost your GPA to get into a "good" high school. The goal was to become better than you were. To truly grow. Out of zero emerged true growth.

"Don't seek to be the best, seek to do your best."

— Sarah-Jane Thomas

Think about all of the areas of life where people are in competition with one another. No matter what lesson we might try to convey to our students in our classroom, especially when it comes to things like grades, class rank, or athletic competition — or anything that you could possibly use to compare people, there is a constant competitive nature. Students feel defined by numbers and judge their value based on these same numbers. Then they judge their value based on the numbers of classmates. It was the same way when I was in high school, college, and even law school. But what I learned is that to become better, to learn from mistakes, the competition should not be with one's classmates or colleagues. Instead it needs to be with oneself.

We can encourage students to only worry about themselves. We can share quotes of motivation, but at the end of it all, there will still be the thrill or fear of competition. There will always be those who do better than you and worse than you, and if we spend our lives worrying about what everybody else is doing, rather than focusing on ourselves, how can we expect to make progress and be successful in our own unique ways? We need to strive for OUR best, and even if we end up last, knowing we gave it our all is far more valuable. What is the price of competition?

Rodney Turner
Virtual Educator
@TechyTurner

The best. Greatest of all time. Expert. Master. Top Dog. Ruler. Sovereign.

These words denote one who has taken time to hone a skill or a set of skills, to be the one who others look to and say they are the expert for the task at hand.

Every day, millions of hours are spent by people practicing what they find to be a hobby, passion, or just simply something they like to do.

As a young adult, I played auto racing games for hours to be the best with a certain car and on a specific track.

Later, I took hundreds of hours away from my family to learn how to use an Interactive Whiteboard so I could leverage the technology in my classroom.

I spent thousands of hours scanning social media to answer educational questions or comment on instructional strategies which I had used in my classroom.

Why? Because I wanted to be the best at what I did.

However, those were not great ways to hone my driving skills, build my knowledge of edtech tools, or my social media skill set. I needed to prioritize my family, my work, and my hobbies. In the struggle to be the best, I was not doing my best.

A tired father gets home from a long day and neglects the kind word, a smiling face, a loving hug which says, "I love you!" The weekends were times to "decompress" and completely isolate myself from my family, and I was not at my best.

To do my best, I have to take inventory of what I have been given to do, analyze what truly is important to me, and place each item in its proper place in my life. Doing my best means following through on promises made to others. Saying, "No," when there is a schedule conflict, and asking clarifying questions to make sure information is clear.

Doing my best means ordering my life in a way that all of the important people, tasks, and skills are at the forefront.

It is a struggle, but I will gladly continue to do my best.

———

LIKE RODNEY REMINDS US, pushing ourselves too hard comes at a cost. Even if we "win," we may end up losing in the end. There are so many things that we need to keep up with, that finding balance and being present for others can lose out. I find myself often telling students that they don't have to be the best; it's not about that. They simply need to do their best and be okay with that, whether or not they win or lose. It only matters that you did what you could and gave it your all.

SHARE: CHOOSE A QUOTE FROM THE CHAPTER AND SHARE A STORY.

#QUOTES4EDU

MY STUDENTS, CASSY AND CELAINE

Students have as much of an impact on us as we can on them. Looking back over the past five years, I have been fortunate to learn from my students. I have seen tremendous growth in Cassy and Celaine. I'm thankful to have had the opportunity to learn from them and with them. Always willing to help, to lead, and to take risks with learning along the way. And more than that, sharing their love of learning with others. When students have choices in learning and know they are supported, there is no limit to what they can achieve.

Chapter 16

LIGHTS, LEARNING, ACTION

CASSY DEBACCO AND CELAINE HORNSBY

"It is easy to sit up and take notice; what is difficult is getting up and taking action." — Honoré de Balzac

---

The Good and the Bad

(C elaine) Growing up in a small school district, most teachers had a traditional style of teaching: a slideshow presentation with notes, presented to students while they took notes, and occasionally assigned a project in which students were supposed to somehow utilize knowledge that perhaps they never fully understood. This is how it had been for most of my years in school. Don't get me wrong, as a high-achieving student, this style resulted in my academic success because it was easy for me to find loopholes to doing well on tests without studying. A day or so after the test, I could not tell you what I had just learned.

However, this is not the way that learning should be. Students should be able to retain the information they have learned beyond just the day of the test! My way of learning was forever changed when I walked through the door of my seventh grade Spanish I class. I never had a teacher like Mrs. Poth, that taught using different tools besides a SMART board, markers, books, and their brain. Mrs. Poth used different technology tools that encouraged and promoted learning. I was finally able to have a deeper connection with what I was being taught because: 1) I enjoyed learning this way, and 2) I was exposed to knowledge differently. Luckily, other teachers started adopting this new, fun process of teaching and learning.

I (Cassy) have always enjoyed learning. I was always THAT KID who didn't want school to be canceled and never wanted to skip a class for any reason. And I am still THAT KID. My teachers are the ones who have inspired me to become such a curious learner. They have inspired me to WANT to learn more and be the best I can be. They have done that by how they teach. I have been the most inspired in classes where I felt I had control of my learning.

In my Spanish class, we completed projects that we designed as part of our PBL (Project Based Learning), and we had a choice in how we were assessed. Having this control made me feel more excited to learn and do well. In my physics class, it was up to me to reassess to earn a higher grade. It was up to me to do extra practice to understand the material. This was unlike other classes where you take notes, you get homework, you take tests, and that is it. In physics, I had to decide what work I needed to do and when I wanted to take a test to earn my grade. This teaching method prepares me for challenging classes in the future and how to handle such challenges. It teaches me how to put my learning and my education in my own hands. This method might not work for everyone, but I felt so in control, and I really wanted to learn. However, not all teachers have inspired me in this way.

I have had my fair share of classes where I feel like I accomplished nothing. I have sat in classes literally counting down the minutes until it was over — not because I was bored or I didn't want to do the work, but because I felt like I wasn't truly learning. The classes where I feel inspired the most are when teachers connect the information we are learning to experiences outside of the classroom, like being able to communicate with students from Spain about Spanish culture, or when I learned how and when different mathematical equations are used in the "real world." As a student, I understand that certain information needs to be taught and a lot of information retained. The difference for me is how that information is presented. Even in my AP chemistry class, I felt inspired. It wasn't because I was good at it. It definitely wasn't because it was easy and MOST DEFINITELY wasn't because I loved chemistry. But I was inspired by how my teacher connected this abstract information to situations that related to me and my life. Not all teachers automatically make an effort to connect the information either; however, it makes a huge difference. It is hard to ask for those connections to be made or for new teaching styles because we are so focused on wondering "why am I not understanding this content" that we feel frustrated that the current style isn't working.

Children are the Future...

(Celaine)...so why not act like it? Many students may not feel inspired in school because they are not able to decide what they learn. More times than not, teachers determine what the students should learn, and the students oblige. By giving students a say, you are letting them sit behind the wheel of their education. Going along with this analogy, students are more attentive. Giving students a voice can be as simple as letting them choose how they create a project, deciding what they learn in class, or letting them TEACH the class. When students are able to think and speak freely, and are not afraid to unleash their academic potential, they will be at full learning capacity.

(Cassy) Whenever teachers use different techniques and connect learning in innovative ways, it inspires students. We feel more creative, excited and eager to learn. We feel heard and understood. Strong teaching inspires me to be the best student I can be. This means teaching in a way that encourages and shows students that teachers have confidence in them and see their potential. Students can do so much if given a chance. So, give students the chance to be inspired, and you'll see they will strive for the greatness that is deep within them.

Getting Personal

(Celaine) Be the inspiration so students know they matter, and that they aren't just a number in a room full of numbers. I have only started to feel this way beginning with my ninth-grade year when the competition starts to heat up to get good grades for college and achieve a high-class rank. To solve this, take a chance and get to know your students. Try to find what makes them tick and use that to motivate them. They'll want to come to school if they have something to look forward to. Students will be more willing to learn and comprehend deeper if they have a reason, such as the student-educator connection. Be the beacon of light that they often need in their day.

Some teachers in my school have taken the initiative to know me better: they ask how I'm doing and tell me that it is okay to talk to them about what's going on in my life. Because of this bond and feeling more comfortable in school, I find myself trying to pay more attention in their class. They have taken time to get to know me, so I should show the same courtesy by taking time for their class.

(Cassy) The traditional learning style of lecture and notes leaves little room for personal connections. There is no ability to teach to individual students when the style of teaching is the same all the time. Students learn differently. Some are visual learners, some are auditory learners, some are hands-on learners, and the list goes on. When teaching styles are diversified, students are more likely to find a teaching style that they can connect with. All I would ask for is variety because I believe there is something that every student can connect with, if given the opportunity. Diversification of methods enables teachers to connect with students through their style, and for students to connect with teachers and the information. In my English class, our midterm assessment was to complete assignments related to a poet that each student chose. No student had the same poet. As we worked on our assignments, our teacher went around to each student, asking about the poet and offering suggestions to help us as we completed our work. Our teacher made an effort to use techniques and provide help that suited each student individually with their assessments and created personal connections in the classroom. Not all teachers may have time to visit with each student in the class, but by using different kinds of teaching, they can still create personal connections.

Every day in my Tech Ed class in ninth grade, we seemed to be learning differently: we took notes, watched videos, did research, watched demonstrations, built items, worked individually or collectively. It made it a very interesting class that I was invested in. I felt connected to the teacher and the information I was learning. The different teaching styles created a sense of comfort almost — I knew there was always something that could help me succeed. Personal connections between students and teachers don't just have to be through a teaching style. Strong teachers are those who learn about their students and genuinely care. A simple "are you doing okay today?" or "let me help you with this" or "you did a great job" show concern and care for students. This helps students feel comfortable and excited to walk into the classroom, ready to learn and to be a part of an encouraging environment.

The Psychology of it All

When teachers are positive, encouraging, creative, and form connections with students, it makes a huge difference in learning. That kind of teaching is what excites students. Classes that give me opportunities to take advantage of my learning are the ones I like the most. These classes are often not textbook-dependent classes and are more flexible. They create more freedom and student choice, which makes me feel more passionate and empowered to learn. Whenever I want to learn, I actually learn more because I am active in my learning and seek help when I need it. I understand and retain information better, and I care about striving to my best. Students are often seen as not trying in school because many students likely just don't care. Going beyond the norm is what inspires students to do their best and be their best. It makes the difference.

(Celaine) I remember one day in my 10th-grade pre-calculus class; my teacher came in acting unusually mean. He usually put on an "act" around students, but this time was different. If you looked close enough, you could see the steam coming out of his ears. I could not pay attention at all during class because I was so shocked that a teacher would act this way: I was honestly on the brink of tears. After insulting our intellect while "teaching" us, he told us there would be a test the next day as we scurried out the door. The rest of the day we could not stop talking about what a terrible mood he was in, and how we would surely fail the test tomorrow since we focused on the insults rather than the content. Later that day, we found out that this was all for a psychology experiment for one of our fellow classmates. Our classmate was testing the theory that teachers' attitude towards students affects their ability to succeed, and she was right! Unfortunately, our class was not able to complete the experiment. However, other results showed that when the teacher was angry and discouraging, the students did worse than students who were exposed to the teacher being kind and encouraging. Sometimes it can be hard to stay positive in the classroom, but as seen by these results, it makes an impact on learning.

Notes. Complain. Process. Repeat.

(Cassy) In school, we tend to have a constant routine that we go through. We go to class, we are lectured at, and we take notes that don't mean anything the moment after we stop writing. It is hard to find meaning in content that is not connected to a bigger picture — knowing things like: What's the goal in learning this piece of information? How does this connect to the overall objectives in the class? How does this relate to the real world? Then, we complain to our friends or really anyone who will listen about how much we hate school and how much we are sick of the boring notes. We go home, we go to sleep, but we have to get up the next day and do it all over again. As students, we complain and complain but don't do anything about it. Many students are scared to speak up; they feel that their opinions aren't valuable and are rarely taken seriously. Students might occasionally offer suggestions of things that they would like to see in the classroom, but those often get overlooked. I have often suggested new ideas, and I was politely shut down. It is hard for teachers to change their methods and there is so much information to cover day-to-day, which is understandable. We are forced into this never-ending cycle. Students don't have a choice in what or how they are taught. We must sit through classes that we are expected to succeed in no matter what. This is how school is, and there aren't many things that can be done to change it. Teachers make a huge difference in a student's experience. As students, we notice this. Everyone notices things that bother them, or that they feel could or should be changed. But how often do things change? More importantly, how often does the world stop complaining and take action?

(Celaine) Last year there was a running joke with this kid in my grade. Every day he came into a class and said, "I hate school." I just laughed at him, until this year I found myself saying the same thing. Maybe it is the senioritis talking, or maybe I am tired of the tedious routine. I walk into first period every day, sit down, and take notes. I turn to my tablemates, complain how much I hate doing this, and go back to taking notes. Oh look, there's the bell! And now to repeat this eight more times and then my day is done. By the end of the day, I have to sit down and process what I have "learned." I find that I spend more time complaining about taking notes than actually comprehending the information I have just written down. Don't get me wrong, I actually learn better by writing information, but after never-ending days of doing the same thing, I get bored from the repetition. This boredom causes my loss of comprehension. I would much rather take notes one day, do an activity the next day that deepens our understanding of the notes, and repeat. Splitting up the routine keeps things interesting and has me constantly wondering, "What are we going to do today?" I might retain more information, but unless there is change brought about, I may never know my full potential.

Opinions: Everybody's Got Them

(Cassy) We all know this. Most people have something that they are passionate about, whether it is related to school, political issues, social issues, sports, art, or something else. There are so many things in the world that lead us to form opinions. And because of this, we as humans take notice of things that fuel our passions. The world is not perfect (shocker, I KNOW). So, there are things that we will take note of that we want to change. This happens all the time. Personally, I get a little upset or even angry at things that I notice every day. I will complain to the person closest to me about it and go about my day. And big surprise, nothing changes. But these opinions make us who we are. They are important and deserve to be heard. However, they will never be heard unless we are intentional and do something about it.

(Celaine) As you may know, many students (especially teenagers) are very opinionated. Even the quiet ones, like myself, have opinions. Even if they don't make them known —although more times than not, students feel like their opinions don't matter because they aren't "old enough" or "smart enough" to know what's going on in the world. Spark a conversation with a student and ask for their opinion. I guarantee their knowledge will shock you. By letting them state their opinions and use their voice, you are feeding into their passion. Using an idea like Project/Problem Based Learning (PBL for short), students are then able to learn more about things that they are passionate about and interested in. I personally like doing this because I am learning about what I want, not what the state or country requires me to learn.

Actions Speak Louder Than Words

(Cassy) This is well known, and it makes sense. We can complain all we want, but until we take action and speak our mind, nothing will ever change. One example of this is when the students in my school took action toward the school board. When our school board planned to make changes to our school district to fix our debt and budget, students joined together and stood in solidarity to voice their concerns and opinions before the school board. We noticed something, and we acted. And even though it might not have gone our way, we learned the importance of speaking up and standing up for ourselves. No matter how important, it doesn't make it easy. Doing what is right isn't always easy, which is why it is important to do it, to speak up and take action for your passions and opinions.

For the past few years, I had the opportunity to attend and speak at local and state edtech conferences. I was sharing the things that I am passionate about. Now, I am writing chapters in books to share my passions and opinions about education, teaching and technology, teaching. Speaking out doesn't always have to be negative. You can share positive experiences to encourage others to do the same. I had the chance to present the same presentation I did at those conferences to some of my teachers. I was honored to speak about my passions and share all I had learned about tech tools to enhance learning. I am proud that I have taken advantage of the opportunities presented to me where I could share my knowledge. I really do believe I can make a difference.

(Celaine) I would not consider myself the type of person to stand up and act out of my own free will; I would rather sit back and take everything in than fight for something I care about. It is hard for me to do, but it is a crucial part of learning. When I have to stand up in class and present in front of my peers (one of the most terrifying experiences for me), I have to be knowledgeable. If I don't know what I am talking about, it is harder to put myself out there and easier to feel judged by peers. When I am presenting on something that I care about, it is a little easier to set aside my fears and just do it.

In my civics class, a discussion popped up about the government, as it usually does. Our teacher told a story about how one of his neighbors (who did not vote) always complained about how terrible the government was. My teacher basically told the person "you have no right to complain, if you don't do anything to improve the situation, i.e., voting!" This really stuck with me. Be willing to do something about it! Applying this to learning, be willing to change how you learn. Find new tools that really stick with you, and help you grow as a student and a person. Be willing to change how you teach. Listen to students' needs and wants as a learner and make learning fun! With intentional planning and collaboration, anything is possible.

Where do we go from here?

In conclusion, I urge teachers to continue to have faith and confidence in their students. I believe in the power of learning, in having an education, and the difference it can make in a student's life. It is so important to teach students in a way that inspires them to act and go forward to do great things. So here are my final thoughts, as a current student to any teacher: Be creative in the classroom. Take risks to enhance learning. Be supportive. Make connections. Create opportunities. Encourage and inspire.

But most importantly, I would like to say thank you. Thank you for making a difference. Keep making a difference.

CASSY DEBACCO IS a senior at Riverview High School in Pennsylvania. She is involved in many clubs such as National Honor Society, Students Against Destructive Decisions, Key Club, Spanish Club, Student Council, and holds multiple leadership roles. Cassy is also involved in Varsity Tennis, playing the viola in many groups, and volunteering her time as youth ministry leader. She has presented at edtech conferences such as PAECT, TRETC, and PETE&C. After high school, she plans to continue her education with a major in mathematics.

• • •

CELAINE HORNSBY IS a senior at Riverview High School. She is involved with activities such as Marching/Concert Band, Tennis Team, National Honor Society, Key Club, Spanish Club, and many more. Celaine also has attended and presented at multiple technology conferences at the local and state levels. Next year, she will attend Baylor University to study mechanical engineering.

MY FRIENDSHIP WITH LAURA

I knew Laura through different chats on Twitter, but we became more connected through a book study on Voxer. We are both members of the #4OCFPLN. Laura has so much to share and has been a source of inspiration and constant support for students, educators, family, and friends. I am thankful to have her on this journey with me and for all that I have learned from her.

Chapter 17

"JUST BREATHE."

LAURA STEINBRINK

"When people ask me what the most important thing is in life, I answer: 'Just breathe.'" — Yoko Ono

---

I presented at GRITC (Gulf Regional Innovative Teaching Conference) in July of 2018, and after watching Dave Burgess knock the keynote out of the park, I presented my first session and then attended others. Without knowing what I was getting myself into, I attended a session on mindfulness, and the presenter was a yoga instructor and an elementary teacher. She used breathing techniques and yoga moves with her students to help them self-regulate. I ordered the cute yoga cards that she suggested and pondered the implications for my high school students. Sure, elementary students loved doing the different breathing techniques, but would high school? How could I sell it to them as something that may seem cheesy at first but will help them? Then I remembered Dave's keynote. If I truly feel it is important for students, then why wouldn't I try to teach it to them? Could I find a way to connect my students to this very important content? Yes, yes, I could, and so the Social Emotional Learning (SEL) journey for me began.

Getting Started

Before teaching students what to do, I had to learn the breathing techniques, the strategies for different social-emotional needs, and an idea of where to start. I needed to present with confidence, whatever strategy I started with, and in order to sell it to students as a viable tool in their belts, I had to know it inside and out...ish. I began researching and writing about SEL and observing my students more closely than ever before. While there are a lot of ways to incorporate SEL into the classroom, I tried a breathing technique first. I did a few whole class deep breathing exercises during my Adviser/Advisee (AA) time, and then I also began to quietly target students who frequently worked themselves up into an emotional frenzy, making it difficult for the class and themselves to focus on learning.

Know Your Students

I work hard to build relationships with my students, all of my students. There is a line between having a solid relationship with students and just being nosey or too familiar, but that path needs to be traveled, despite the risk. With that in mind, I set about to invest in knowing the students in my district as early as possible. I try to learn their names while doing my hall supervision at my door between class periods. Middle school students have to pass my door on the way to art, so while high fiving or fist bumping my 12-year-old son and his friends as they pass me in the hall, I engage others in friendly banter. By the time students cross into my room as my own students, I know the names of over half of them on day one if I stay diligent at my hall relationship building.

When AJ entered my classroom as a sophomore, I knew he would be one of those student leaders who I needed to understand early on, and who I wanted to invest time in getting to know as well. I worked all of the first semester building a relationship with him and then the unthinkable happened.

Meet AJ

As a sophomore in my English 2 class, AJ was very bright, funny, and supremely confident in his beliefs. He played on the school's basketball team, had a lot of friends, good grades, and was popular. Even with all of that, AJ was not exactly easy going. His temper was on a short leash and sometimes escaped before his thought process could catch it again. He could also be loud, disruptive, and caught up in the moment. I made sure to keep him engaged in the content while watching for signs of discord between all students in general, and AJ in particular. With a strong personality like his, I wanted to make sure he used his powers for good.

His Story

Yes, I am using past tense. These were my thoughts and actions before AJ's car accident, one he almost didn't walk away from, in fact. A typical day, basketball practice, and then near death just a couple miles from school. AJ was put on a helicopter and rushed to one of the larger hospitals in our area. We had tense hours of waiting for news, and when it did arrive, relief that he had survived washed over us. He fractured a vertebrae in his neck and would require a neck brace for a while. He was, based on the placement of the fracture, a quarter of an inch from never walking again. But more disturbingly, he had suffered a TBI (Traumatic Brain Injury) and short-term memory loss. He needed physical therapy to help his brain remember how to do the things we take for granted. Fortunately, AJ's determination helped his brain remember things quickly, and before the basketball season had ended, he was back on the court in uniform. AJ was back in the game. He was not, however, back to his old self.

The Struggle

AJ did not remember things. He forgot who some people were, forgot things he just said and then repeated them, and while that was funny to his friends some of the time, it was never funny to AJ. He didn't like knowing that he couldn't remember things. Test-taking became a nightmare. He struggled in areas he never had before, and his frustration grew. Thankfully, systems were put in place to give AJ the space to heal as he worked through his new reality. I sat with him as he took my word root tests, helping him stay focused from one question to the next. And if those weren't enough for him to battle, his temper reared its ugly head when he least expected it. The short leash was totally gone now. Without warning and often without provocation, AJ's temper would come to life and leave him helpless for a few minutes as it won the war over his self-control. The TBI came with a pretty high price for AJ to pay, and part of that was a big dent in his impulse control.

The second semester of AJ's sophomore year became a battle-ground. I made sure that he had support in place while in my room, and things did get better as his brain healed. This was one of those times where the wise words of Dave Burgess from the summer keynote kept echoing in the chambers of my mind. We are in the life-changing business. If I had only known then what I know now, I could have given him more tools to self-regulate through those tough times. Know better. Do better.

Moving Forward

Well, he's a junior now and doing very well compared to last spring. More importantly, I know better. High time I start doing better. As I put together blog posts after researching and culling through information on SEL strategies that are easy to implement and will work with all grade levels, I pondered and experimented. A very easy but important strategy stood out above all the rest for me to dip my toe into the SEL waters — deep breaths. It's no secret that deep breathing is nature's best anti-stress medicine. It has stood the test of time as an old wives' tale, primarily because there is some very powerful science behind why it is effective. One analogy used by Matthew MacKinnon M.D. in *Psychology Today* describes it as a biological brake that can help lead to resilience and happiness.

"...in a state of petroleum-fueled anxiety, there is no better remedy than a biological brake."

Biological brake. I saw immediate applications for that. Looking over at AJ during my AA period right before lunch one day, I saw his temper begin to bubble around the edges. Making up my mind to dive in right there, I walked over and got between AJ and the students he was talking to, loudly. I knew he wasn't mad at them but he was telling a story, and clearly one that upset him. I stood my ground in front of him and said his name softly, firmly, and repeatedly until he switched his gaze from his friends behind me to me. Eyes locked with his, quietly, I repeated his name.

"AJ." He finally responded.

"Yes?"

"AJ. Just breathe."

"What?"

"Breathe, AJ. Take a deep breath." He looked at me, puzzled, but did as I asked. I am that teacher who makes students do weird things all the time, so it wasn't a big deal for him to be compliant right then and humor me. He took a deep breath. I had him hold it for a few seconds, let it out slowly and count to four or five while doing so, then repeat. We did this a couple times, and he visibly calmed down. Success. I went on about my business, and he rejoined his friends. This whole episode took only a few minutes, and to students around us, looked just like we were having a quiet, unremarkable conversation. It was quiet, but I walked away doing a tiny happy dance in the depths of my soul. Something simple worked this time. Encouraged, I kept at it.

Round Two

Another student in one of my sophomore English classes tends to get worked up when talking to me. I know part of his back story, so I had suspicions of why he tends to get amped up when I am not teaching the way he prefers, or when I change up the order we do things, or if I don't have a paper activity planned. While he isn't always disruptive or loud, he can be. It starts at the beginning of class and my reactions to his occasional quiet condescending anger, pushing his 6'2" frame inside my personal space bubble, to determine how class will go for him the rest of the hour. Equipped with the simple, quiet command to breathe that worked with AJ, I watched this student carefully during the next few days. Then it happened. He towered over me as I greeted students at my door one day, demanding to know what we were going to be doing, and as I answered, I could see the tension and anger bubbling. I stopped in mid-sentence, looked up at him, and quietly but firmly, said his name. For purposes of this book, I'll call him John (as in Doe).

"John."

"I don't understand why we can't…" I interrupted him.

"John."

"What?" I heard and felt the unhappiness. Anger. Here we go.

"John, just breathe." He looked at me, thinking. I pressed forward.

"Breathe. Take a big breath in slowly. Let it out slowly. Count to four or five as you breathe in and as you breathe out." I was quietly giving instructions as students swirled passed us into my room and back out again to go to the restroom, locker, or to tell their friend or significant other one last thing before the tardy bell rang. I stayed locked in eye contact with John. His nose flared but his facial expressions eased back into a more relaxed look. He gave me a short nod and entered the classroom. Huh. Nonplussed, I finished greeting students, waving those in need of the bathroom to hurry, then closed the door when the bell rang, and the last student had made it back to the room. Class began. John was fine the whole hour.

Small Steps

These two small successes may seem trivial, but they were huge in helping those two students cool themselves down in those two moments. Could I do more? Would this work again? Yes, and yes. I allow students to get a drink at the fountain or fill up their water bottles nearly any time during class except when I am giving directions or direct instruction. No hassles. Water is important for their brains and bodies, and it is an easy SEL strategy to be mindful of during the day. Movement, thanks to the book *Teach Like a Pirate* (Burgess), was already involved in my learning experiences, but I use it more now for quick brain breaks and a couple minutes of refocusing between activities too.

But most importantly, my radar is honed in to students having trouble with an overflow of those explosive emotions. I follow the same process each time, and I never make a scene while doing it. I don't call that student out in class or in any way draw attention to our quiet breathing sessions...er...moments. Each time John starts to lecture me about what we're doing in class that displeases him, I listen. If I see that his temper is gaining momentum, I stop him in mid-rant. I tell him to breathe. It hasn't failed me yet, but I know there are other strategies I can use when it does fail me.

A Defining Moment

During my fourth-hour prep period, I can have anywhere from zero to four of my yearbook students come to hang out in my room. Since installing flexible seating last year, I've learned to let go of that urge to control my space as if it were mine and mine alone. It's not. So if these students get permission from their lab classes, classes my district set up for students to have a seated period during the school day to work on assignments from online college classes or to take online high school classes —whether as credit recovery or to get a credit we don't offer in a seated class, they can come to my room. My yearbook students get their work done while relaxing in my room, but I don't let others invade our time. That is, I didn't, until AJ walked in one day, a few weeks after our first breathing moment. The knock at the door is always annoying because none of us want to stop what we're doing to answer it, but on this day, I got up and answered it. AJ walked in, clearly upset. He began telling the three students I had in there about what upset him, and I knew what I had to do. I walked over, got between him and his audience, opened my mouth to speak, and he slid his eyes to mine.

"I know, Mrs. Steinbrink. I'm going to breathe. In fact, I was getting so upset in there that I had to leave before I got really mad."

"Good, AJ. Does your teacher know you are here?

"Oh yeah. I told him I had to come to your room to breathe." A little stunned, I just looked at him.'

"So, it works?" You see, we hadn't discussed anything. I didn't explain what I was doing. I just had him stop and breathe.

"Yes! It's really helping!" Well. Huh.

I could have chosen to hit the beach instead of attending that small session on mindfulness in Alabama at the Gulf Regional Innovative Teaching Conference. I didn't, and because of that, I helped AJ. That biological brake that all of us can use when we begin to feel overwhelmed, angry, stressed and on edge has become a lifeline for him to use when the residual effects of his TBI surface. He's learning to walk off his emotions. To breathe. Just breathe.

LAURA STEINBRINK, a teacher for 23 years, presents technology and instructional practices at workshops locally, around her state, and nationally. She is also the Communications Director and Webmaster for the Plato R-V School District. Laura is the author of www.rockntheboat.com, a Feedspot Top 200 blog in Education. She has published articles for Matt Miller, author of Ditch That Textbook and Co-Author of Ditch That Homework with Alice Keeler; Denis Sheeran, author of Instant Relevance; and various articles for other educational related companies.

Chapter 18

LESSONS LEARNED

"Connected learners need connected leaders."

— Mark Carbone and Donna Fry

L ooking back over my teaching career, I wish I knew the power of being connected from the very beginning. The first step we must take is to break away from any isolation that we might have placed ourselves in, whether by choice or by consequence. As George Couros says, "isolation is now a choice educators make." It is time to make a different choice. As educators, we are constantly surrounded by and connected to others. Each day we have the opportunity to interact with students, colleagues, administrators, parents, or members of the community, in the physical or virtual space. We are, by default, connected to the others with whom we interact each day. But without spending time beyond a class period or the school day, our connections only exist superficially.

What I mean is that we might talk, share ideas, and have laughs together during the school day, but are we intentionally connecting with colleagues outside of the school space? Realistically, how much extra time do we have to really get to know one another during the school day? Are there plans to get together for something fun, is time set aside to co-plan for classes? Are you learning more about your colleagues than just their basic information? Think about how often you have conversations with colleagues during the week. You probably pass by many of them each day in the hall (if you are escaping the isolation of your classroom), but time only permits for a quick hello or a smile, if even that. How many times do you pass by and there is not even eye contact made between you? Is everyone so busy that we don't have time to slow down, to pause to engage with colleagues and break away from what can be an isolating existence for teachers in the school? Do we avoid eye contact because we are afraid to get pulled into a conversation? We should not be. Even small moments help to build critical relationships.

"We all understand the importance of asking for help; Those who achieve big things are the ones who accept it when it's offered."

— *Simon Sinek*

There is a difference in wanting to stay isolated because it is more comfortable. It can be more of a personal preference — there is a lot of work that needs to be done, and there never seems to be enough time. But it is entirely different if there are not opportunities to connect and worse, if there is little if any awareness of how to become connected. Every day as we work with our students, the goal is to support them and to help them develop the skills that they will need for whatever their future holds. We cannot predict with any amount of accuracy, but the likelihood is that they will need to turn to others in the future whether it be to ask for help, to share ideas, to work together in the same space, or to collaborate on a task virtually. While in school, teachers are the best source of information and learning available to the students. Of course, students have access to electronic devices and numerous choices in virtual assistants, but being able to talk directly to a real person and work through the learning process together is far more beneficial than learning that happens through static information delivered on a device any day.

The best way to prepare students is by helping them to connect and collaborate with peers and to reach out into and learn about their community. "Connected learners need connected leaders" (Mark Carbone and Donna Fry). It starts with us. We must be prepared to do something different, to put ourselves out there so we can be the best version of ourselves for our students. To be better tomorrow, than we are today. Even if we prefer to work alone in our room and avoid the faculty lounges at all costs, and we are okay with that, we need to find a way to be okay with doing the opposite sometimes. It's not about us. Isolating ourselves, in turn, isolates students from a world full of opportunities. We close ourselves off to wonderful learning experiences beyond our classroom, our own knowledge and skills.

Time is short. Finding extra minutes in the day rarely happens, which is why we need other options that provide access and time to connect. I find it is easier to connect with educators from around the world. As big of a task as that may seem, it's really quite simple. A world that is so big can suddenly feel so small when you realize the power of connecting and the impact it has on your personal and professional growth. More important is the impact you will have on students.

My Escape from Isolation

I wanted to know everything, but I didn't know where to begin. My hesitancy to connect on any social media platforms and my habit of isolating myself in my room or in the teacher work center did not help me to find my way. Throughout this book, you heard from many educators with different backgrounds and experiences. In seeking stories to share, I had no idea of the impact it would have on me as I wrote this book. Knowing these educators, people who have become my friends, and still some of whom I have never met in person, has helped me to grow personally and professionally. And more importantly, being connected has given me the courage to take risks, the motivation to do more, and the knowledge that I am not alone. If I had not taken a chance by connecting through Facebook, then Twitter, and eventually Voxer, I very likely would still be teaching in isolation. And worse, my students would be isolated from a world full of opportunities to grow.

I have become "connected" through several PLNs. My first true PLN is referred to as the "53s," a group based on trust, transparency, empathy, kindness, pushback, fun and passion for education and the power of learning, and most importantly, true friendship. My 53s are: Evan Abramson, Jarod Bormann, Jennifer Casa-Todd, Jaime Donally, Mandy Froehlich, Tisha Richmond and Rodney Turner.

Sometimes a PLN forms in unique ways. I had joined a Voxer book study of *The Four O'clock Faculty* (2017) by Rich Czyz. When the book study ended in January 2018, many members of the group stayed connected and kept the conversation going. Today we are connected in the #4OCFPLN and many of the writers in this book are members of this PLN.

I am proud to know these educators and call them my friends. My 53s and the #4OCFPLN have provided more knowledge, inspiration and support, than I could have ever imagined possible.

I'm thankful each day for the support they have given to me and that we have given to one another. There are many lessons that I have learned along the way to get me where I am today and inspire me to improve for the future. Most of what I have learned has come about from being a more connected educator.

These educators are a positive force in my life.

Once we *Believe* In *Ourselves*
We can risk curiosity, wonder, spontaneous delight, or any experience that reveals the human spirit.

E.E. Cummings

@SteinbrinkLaura

"Once we believe in ourselves, we can risk curiosity, wonder, spontaneous delight, or any experience that reveals the human spirit." — E.E. Cummings

We learn and grow by telling our stories, sharing our perspectives, and making ourselves vulnerable. I am better today than I was yesterday because of a supportive PLN and a newfound willingness to take risks, fail, and try again. I often hear others ask, "What story could I tell? What would make mine any different?" My response is always that although we may have similar experiences, successes, or failures, we walk away with a different perspective and a unique lesson learned.

I am humbled by all of the educators, my friends, who joined this journey with me. With each story I read or heard, it pushed me to reflect on my own practice and provided me with different lenses through which to view my students and my classroom. I know their purpose for doing what they do, and I know their passion. I know what these educators and storytellers stand for, and finally, feel like I belong. It simply took one step to break away from isolation and not look back.

"*Everyone who got to where they are had to begin where they are.*"
— *Richard Paul Evans*

Kristen Nan
Educator
Pittsburgh, PA
@nankr1120

To know where you are going, you must stop and look at
where you are, not to mention where you have come from. If
there is one thing that life has taught me, it is that you
cannot go around, instead you must go through — and
doing it together creates a world of possibility. Each of us
has had a starting point. That point may have been a traditional mindset or possibly a risk-taking, vulnerable, open
mind that was ready for change. Either way, we started at a
point that would now be less than innovative if we were still
there at this very moment. When I stop and think about
where I am in education today, I sit in awe at the changes
that have come about. Some were by choice, while others

were not so much. When it is all said and done, none of the changes could have occurred if others would not have met me where I was at in my edulife.

At times I was well ahead of the game, needing a small push in the right direction. At other times, I needed more of a shove as my version of "personal best" fell short of what my students deserved. The fact of the matter is, if we don't know where one is at, or if we do not take the time to build a relationship to know the mindset of others, we cannot possibly move forward. Life does not gift you growth. It may gift you tangible objects that add up as "stuff," but if we want personal gain… the kind that creates endless possibilities, we must work hard. We must choose to better ourselves. We must hold ourselves accountable and then push ourselves beyond our own version of "best." Then, and only then, can we sit in wonder of life's impact on where we are at… because the only way we got here, "was to begin where we were at."

I AM A PART OF EVERYTHING I HAVE READ.
TEDDY ROOSEVELT

I AM a part of everything that I have read and the lessons I've learned from my PLN. I am not the same teacher I was when I started teaching, nor writing this book, and I am not the same as I was yesterday. I am, and always will be, a work in progress. I learn as I go. Each day I will strive to make a difference for my students, to push myself to go beyond what I think I am capable of and take one more step. I might fall down, as I have before, but I will get right back up and try again.

My purpose is to encourage students to not give up, to dream big, to be okay with falling and failing, and to always know they have someone cheering them on. In the words of the late Rita Pierson, "Every child needs a champion." Today is your day. Be a champion for students and learning. DARE to be different. Dream, Advocate, Risk, Empower.

Music, Motivations, and More

Quotes lead me to think about life and learning, and sometimes fuel me with energy to do more. Music has a similar effect on me. Music can inspire us to act, provide calmness amid chaos, create an escape, and if only temporarily, bring back memories and lift our spirits when we need it the most. Sometimes it just takes the right song, the right lyrics, to make a difference. Everyone needs to have a theme song, or a pick me up song. Because I do not make decisions easily, I have five songs that bounce around in my mind and instantly lift me up, and when I play music between classes, it lifts students up too. My five are *High Hopes*, *Whatever it Takes*, *Unwritten*, *Good Morning*, and *Shoot Straight*. If I took the specific lyrics that lift me up and made a new song, my mixed theme song would become:

> It's a brand-new day, Ain't no clouds hanging
>> over me
> Something doesn't feel the same, the rest of my life
>> gonna start today
> Had to have high hopes for a living didn't know how
>> but I always had a feeling,
> I break tradition, sometimes my tries, are outside the
>> lines

We've been conditioned to not make mistakes, but I
    can't live that way
Everybody hoping they could be the one, I was born
    to run, I was born for this
Whatever you do, do with all your heart, and
    wherever you go, you'll go far.
Today is where your book begins
The rest is still unwritten

Have a Theme Song

Panic at the Disco
Had to have high hopes for a living didn't know how
    but I always had a feeling, I was gonna be that one
    in a million always had high, high hopes.

Max Frost
Baby it's a brand-new day, Ain't no clouds hanging
    over me
Something doesn't feel the same, the rest of my life
    gonna start today

Imagine Dragons
Falling too fast to prepare for this, Tripping in the
    world could be dangerous
Everybody circling, it's vulturous, Negative, nepotist
Everybody waiting for the fall of man, Everybody
    praying for the end of times
Everybody hoping they could be the one,
I was born to run, I was born for this

JT Lewis
Whatever you do, do with all your heart, and
    wherever you go, you'll go far.
Don't be afraid to cry, don't forget to laugh

Natasha Bedingfield
I break tradition, sometimes my tries, are outside the
    lines
We've been conditioned to not make mistakes, but I
    can't live that way...
Today is where your book begins
The rest is still unwritten

SHARE: WHAT IS YOUR THEME SONG? LET'S CREATE A PLAYLIST!

#QUOTES4EDU

IMAGE CREDITS

When I reached out to my PLN for graphics for the quotes this book, I never imagined the response that I would get. I'm so thankful for the beautiful and unique contributions and their willingness to be a part of this writing journey.

Michael Mordechai Cohen @TheTechRabbi
Dene Gainey @Dene_gainey
Manuel Herrera @ManuelHerrera
Shelby Krevokuch
Dana Ladenburger @dladenburger
Heather Lippert @msyoung114
Amber McCormick @EdTechAmber
Scott Nunes @MrNunesTeach
Tisha Richmond @TishRich
Chris Spalton @ChrisSpalton
Monica Spillman @mospillman
Laura Steinbrink @SteinbrinkLaura
Kitty Tripp @Kitty_Tripp
Julie Woodard @Woodard_Julie

REFERENCES

Barshay, J. (2019). Two studies point to the power of teacher-student relationships to boost learning. Retrieved from https://hechingerreport.org/two-studies-point-to-the-power-of-teacher-student-relationships-to-boost-learning/

Blume, J. (1970). Are you there God? It's me, Margaret. New York, NY: Random House. Grant, A. M., & Sandberg, S. (2016). Originals: How non-conformists move the world. New York, New York: Viking.

Bond, M. (1958). A Bear Called Paddington. London: HarperCollins Children's Books.

Bond, M. (1981). Paddington goes to town, Harper Collins.

Brown, B. (2018). Dare to lead: Brave work, tough conversations, whole hearts. New York: Random House.

Brown, B. (2015). Daring Greatly: How the Courage to be Vulnerable Transforms the Way We Live, Love, Parent, and Lead. London, England: Penguin Books.

Burgemeester, A. (2016, October 19). Jean Piaget's Theory of Play.

Retrieved January 10, 2019, from https://www.psychologized.org/jean-piagets-theory-of-play/

Burgess, D. (2012). Teach Like A Pirate. San Diego, CA: Dave Burgess Consult8ing.

Casas, J. (2017). Culturize: Every student, every day, whatever it takes. San Diego, CA: Dave Burgess Consulting, Incorporated.

Centers for Disease Control and Prevention (2016). Adverse Childhood Experiences (ACEs). Retrieved from https://bit.ly/2BH4ncO

Coda, R., & Jetter, R. (2016). Escaping the School Leader's Dunk Tank: How to prevail when others want to see you drown. San Diego, CA: Dave Burgess Consulting.

Couros, G. (2015). The Innovator's Mindset: Empower Learning, Unleash Talent, and Lead a Culture of Creativity. San Diego, CA: Dave Burgess Consulting.

Couros, G. (2019, January 24). The Importance of Isolation in a Highly Connected World. Retrieved January 29, 2019, from https://georgecouros.ca/blog/archives/tag/isolation-is-a-choice-educators-make

Czyz, R. (2017). The Four O'clock Faculty: A rogue guide to revolutionize professional development. San Diego, CA: Dave Burgess Consulting.

DeWitt, P. (2014, November 08). 5 Reasons We Need Instructional Coaches. Retrieved from https://blogs.edweek.org/edweek/finding_common_ground/2014/11/5_reasons_we_need_instructional_coaches.html

Dweck, C. S. (2008) Mindset: The New Psychology of Success New York: Ballantine Books.

Falecki, D. (2017). Impact on Students. Retrieved March 8, 2019, from http://www.teacher-wellbeing.com.au/research/impact-on-students/

Fastiggi, W., & Fastiggi, W. (2014). Will Fastiggi. Retrieved January 20, 2019, from https://technologyforlearners.com/summary-of-john-hatties-research/

Fisk, P. (2017, April). Moonshot Thinking [PDF]. The Genius Works. https://www.thegeniusworks.com/wp-content/uploads/2017/04/Moonshot-Thinking-by-Peter-Fisk-.pdf

Fulghum, R. (2004). All I need to know I learned in kindergarten: Uncommon thoughts on common things. New York, NY: Ballantine Books.

Hattie, J. (2010). Visible learning: A synthesis of over 800 meta-analyses relating to achievement. London: Routledge.

Jost, J., & Hunyady, O. (2003). The psychology of system justification and the palliative function of ideology. *European review of social psychology, 13*(1), 111-153.

Killian, S. (2017, September 24). Hattie's 2017 Updated List of Factors Influencing Student Achievement. Retrieved March 8, 2019, from http://www.evidencebasedteaching.org.au/hatties-2017-updated-list/

Knight, J. (2018) "Coaches Need to Affirm the People They Coach, but Also Be Careful Not to Affirm Them Away from Confronting Reality. If My Positive Comments Make It Easier for You to Avoid Reality, I'm Likely Doing It so You'll Think Well of Me, Not Because It Helps You." *Twitter*, Twitter, 27 Dec. 2018, twitter.com/jimknight99/status/1078379197473701888.

Kozol, J. (1991). Savage inequalities: Children in America's Schools. New York, NY: Harper Perennial.

MacKinnon, M. "The Science of Slow Deep Breathing." Psychology Today, Sussex Publishers, 7 Feb. 2016, www.psychologytoday.com/us/blog/neuraptitude/201602/the-science-slow-deep-breathing

National Governors Association Center for Best Practices, Council of Chief State School Officers. (2010). Common Core State Standards for English Language Arts and Mathematics. National Governors Association Center for Best Practices, Council of Chief State School Officers, Washington D.C.

Powell, C. L., & Koltz, T. (2012). It worked for me: In life and leadership. 1st HarperLuxe ed. New York: HarperLuxe.

Readers' Guide to Periodical Literature. (n.d.). Hackensack, NJ: Grey House Publishing.

Rosenthal, R., & Jacobson, L. (1968). Pygmalion in the classroom: Teacher expectation and pupils' intellectual development. New York: Holt, Rinehart, and Winston.

Sanfelippo, J. S. (2017). Hacking Leadership: 10 ways great leaders inspire learning that teachers, students, and parents love. TIMES 10 PUBLICATIONS.

Shakespeare, W., Raffel, B., & Bloom, H. (2005). Macbeth. New Haven: Yale University Press.

Solanki, P. (2018, March 02). Psychology Behind the Golem Effect and Consequences of the Same. Retrieved February 28, 2019, from https://psychologenie.com/psychology-behind-golem-effect

Terada, Y. (2018, September 11). Welcoming Students with a Smile. Retrieved November 10, 2018, from https://www.edutopia.org/article/welcoming-students-smile

Wafula-strike, A. (2010). In my dreams I dance. HarperCollins. p. 79.

Weintraub, J. (Producer) and Soderbergh, S. (Director). 2001. Ocean's Eleven [Motion Picture]. United States: Warner Brothers.

Videos

Couros, G. https://georgecouros.ca/blog/archives/tag/isolation-is-a-choice-educators-make

Google. (2014, May 22). Rubik's Cube: A question, waiting to be answered. Retrieved October 16, 2018, from https://www.youtube.com/watch?v=W1K2jdjLhbo

Songs

Bedingfield, N.; Brisebois, D.; Rodrigues, W. (2004). Unwritten [Recorded by Natasha Bedingfield]. Unwritten [CD]. New York City, New York: Sony Legacy.

Frost, M. (2018). Good morning. [Recorded by Max Frost]. Good Morning. [mp3] Los Angeles, California. Atlantic Records

Imagine Dragons (2017). Whatever it Takes [Recorded by Imagine Dragons]. On Evolve [mp3] Los Angeles, California. KIDinaKO-RNER/Interscope Records

Lewis, J.T., Lynch, S. (2018). Shoot Straight. [Recorded by J.T. Lewis]. Good Times [mp3]. Nashville, Tennessee: Speakeasy Studios

Panic at the Disco (2018). High hopes [Recorded by Panic at the Disco]. Prayer for the Wicked. [CD]. New York City, New York: DCD2 / Fueled by Ramen

ABOUT THE AUTHOR

Rachelle Dene Poth is a longtime French, Spanish and STEAM Teacher and an EdTech Consultant. Rachelle is also an Attorney, has a Master's Degree in Instructional Technology, and serves as President of the ISTE Teacher Education Network and Communications Chair for the Mobile Learning Network. She received the Presidential Gold Award for Volunteer Service to Education in 2018, was selected as One of "20 to watch" by the NSBA and the PAECT Outstanding Teacher of the Year in 2017, and is a Future Ready Instructional Coach. Rachelle is an Edugladiator Core Warrior and an Affiliate of the Pushing Boundaries Consulting LLC.

Rachelle is the author of *The Future is Now* with Edugladiators and one upcoming book project.

She is a contributing author to several books including *EduMatch Snapshot in Education 2016, 2017, 2018* and *Gamify Literacy*, an ISTE publication. She is a regular teacher blogger for DefinedSTEM, Getting Smart, and Kidblog. Rachelle co-moderates #Formativechat on Mondays and maintains her "Learning as I Go" blog site at www.Rdene915.com.

A popular keynote and workshop presenter, Rachelle loves spending time with family and friends and her amazing PLN, the 53s. Follow her on Twitter @Rdene915 and her website.

sites.google.com/view/rachelledenepoth/about-me

OTHER EDUMATCH TITLES

EduMatch Snapshot in Education (2016)
In this collaborative project, twenty educators located throughout the
United States share educational strategies that have worked well for them,
both with students and in their professional practice.

The #EduMatch Teacher's Recipe Guide
Editors: Tammy Neil & Sarah Thomas
*Dive in as fourteen international educators share their recipes for success,
both literally and metaphorically!*

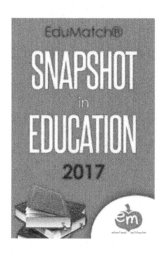

EduMatch Snapshot in Education (2017)
*We're back! EduMatch proudly presents Snapshot in Education (2017). In
this two-volume collection, 32 educators and one student share their tips
for the classroom and professional practice.*

Journey to The "Y" in You by Dene Gainey
This book started as a series of separate writing pieces that were eventually woven together to form a fabric called The Y in You. The question is, "What's the 'why' in you?"

The Teacher's Journey by Brian Costello
Follow the Teacher's Journey with Brian as he weaves together the stories of seven incredible educators. Each step encourages educators at any level to reflect, grow, and connect.

The Fire Within
Compiled and edited by Mandy Froehlich
Adversity itself is not what defines us. It is how we react to that adversity and the choices we make that creates who we are and how we will persevere.

EduMagic by Sam Fecich
This book challenges the thought that "teaching" begins only after certification and college graduation. Instead, it describes how students in teacher preparation programs have value to offer their future colleagues, even as they are learning to be teachers!

Makers in Schools
Editors: Susan Brown & Barbara Liedahl
The maker mindset sets the stage for the Fourth Industrial Revolution,
empowering educators to guide their students.

Divergent EDU by Mandy Froehlich
The concept of being innovative can be made to sound so simple. But what
if the development of the innovative thinking isn't the only roadblock?

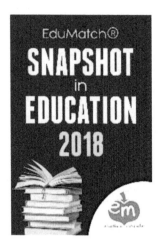

EduMatch Snapshot in Education (2018)
EduMatch® is back for our third annual Snapshot in Education. Dive in as 21 educators share a snapshot of what they learned, what they did, and how they grew in 2018.

Daddy's Favorites by Elissa Joy
Illustrated by Dionne Victoria
Five-year-old Jill wants to be the center of everyone's world. But, her most favorite person in the world, without fail, is her Daddy. But Daddy has to be Daddy, and most times that means he has to be there when everyone needs him, especially when her brother Danny needs him.

Level Up Leadership by Brian Kulak
Gaming has captivated its players for generations and cemented itself as a fundamental part of our culture. In order to reach the end of the game, they all need to level up.

DigCit Kids edited by Marialice Curran & Curran Dee
This book is a compilation of stories, starting with our own mother and son story, and shares examples from both parents and educators on how they embed digital citizenship at home and in the classroom.

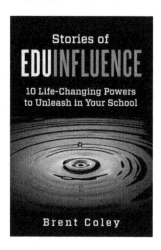

Stories of EduInfluence by Brent Coley
In Stories of EduInfluence, veteran educator Brent Coley shares stories from more than two decades in the classroom and front office, stories illustrating the life-changing power we possess.

The Edupreneur by Dr. Will
The Edupreneur is a 2019 documentary film that takes you on a journey into the successes and challenges of some of the most recognized names in K-12 education consulting.